# War of the Bloods in My Veins

## A STREET SOLDIER'S MARCH TOWARD REDEMPTION

Dashaun "Jiwe" Morris

*All poems by Jason Davis*

SCRIBNER

New York   London   Toronto   Sydney

SCRIBNER
A Division of Simon & Schuster, Inc.
1230 Avenue of the Americas
New York, NY 10020

Copyright © 2008 by Dashaun Morris

First Scribner trade paperback edition September 2009

SCRIBNER and design are registered trademarks of
The Gale Group, Inc., used under license
by Simon & Schuster, Inc., the publisher of this work.

For information about special discounts for bulk purchases,
please contact Simon & Schuster Special Sales at
1-866-506-1949 or business@simonandschuster.com.

The Simon & Schuster Speakers Bureau can bring authors to
your live event. For more information or to book an event,
contact the Simon & Schuster Speakers Bureau at 1-866-248-3049
or visit our website at www.simonspeakers.com.

DESIGNED BY KYOKO WATANABE
Text set in Granjon

Manufactured in the United States of America

1   3   5   7   9   10   8   6   4   2

Library of Congress Control Number: 2007045861

ISBN 978-1-4165-4846-1
ISBN 978-1-4165-4851-5 (pbk)
ISBN 978-1-4165-6533-8 (eBook)

*For Meggette and for Da-Shana*

# War of
# the Bloods
# in My Veins

# Introduction

"You think I bang 'cause I want to? I bang because the gang was my family when I couldn't find Moms and didn't know Dad; I bang because the streets were my school when my teacher wouldn't teach me; and when I had no loot, the game showed me how to take care of those I love. You want me to stop bangin' . . . give me what I was supposed to have from birth . . . love, opportunity, shit . . . not just a hood . . . a community." I heard these profound words from a young brother in Cleveland, Ohio, in 1992 when I, as a college student, was shadowing a local activist doing work with gang members during the truce of the early nineties. It was the first time I had a real window into the humanity behind the headlines. The first time I had interaction with real men and women and not hyped up caricatures of young delinquents. It was the day that the lights came on and I saw that the true condition so many young people were in was bigger than saying no to drugs and yes to school.

The condition so many U.S. cities have created is an environment that seems hopeless and has forced young people to fend for themselves. In my work as the National Youth Director of the NAACP and as a journalist with BET, I have since seen young people that are brilliant but feel like they have nothing to live for. And I have come across young adults that possess all the skills and talents that could take them on the road to their purpose, but they are so angry and depressed that they don't know their own worth. Couple that with the fact that so many of the solutions to engage these same young people that come from government, social, and civic organizations, and even the church, are simply recycled ideas that didn't work the first time, and it makes even the most optimistic of us wonder what the future will hold for such dark times.

But every now and then a light shines through the darkness and provides the kind of transparent testimony and real-life solutions that change the game and provide real triumph after tribulation. This was the light I experienced the first time I met brother Jiwe at an event PR extraordinaire Terrie Williams sponsored for her book dealing with African Americans and depression. I was taken by how open he was willing to be about the experiences of street life that we seldom hear. I, and I know you, have often heard the story of coming up in the rough streets, dealing with drug and gang life and finding redemption after jail, the death of a friend, or the birth of a child. However, that wasn't the keynote of his talk. It was a self-psychological evaluation, diagnosis, and treatment recommendation that was not only honest but also powerful. He spoke of the great depression that he and so many of the soldiers that are still in the game face on a daily basis. He dealt with the almost social schizophrenia that exists when you are trying to survive and the very real emotional turmoil that creates an internal war for the soul that so many of our young people are dealing with.

Jiwe's words during that event only scratched the surface of what he is going to take you through in this book. This is not a book for the faint of heart, or those only looking for a feel-good story of bad kid turned good. Jiwe provides the social commentary that goes beyond the pedagogical theory of the academy and provides real insight into the reasons why fear, insecurity, and isolation are driving so many of our young people to the streets, gangs, and drugs. Additionally, through his own story he illustrates that not all bad kids start off bad. But more important than anything else, Jiwe gives us a window into his most venerable feelings. Challenging the conventional methodology of the street story that requires redemption, but not emotional transparency. He thus gives you the ability to see what he truly struggled with in the innermost workings of his soul, versus just chronicling the street activities he participated in. It's because of this approach that you are able to travel with him through his journey of discovering what he truly had to offer the world, and his fight to then save his own life from himself.

This book will scare you with its gritty reality of life in urban America, and inspire you with the charismatic genius of the author's transformation. But in case you miss it, this is only part one. For this brilliant story does not sell you the wolf ticket that it is all over. The life that Jiwe has yet to live is the sequel that I am looking forward to: how he walks out this new life, raises his kids, and inspires his boys still in the game. *War of the Bloods in My Veins* is the story of the pain he went through, the struggle to challenge his demons, and the ultimate rebirth of Dashaun "Jiwe" Morris. And it gives us a model for the rebirth of a nation of young warriors looking to live a life of true purpose. This book gives us a model of how to win their wars as well. Read it and be empowered.

—JEFF JOHNSON
NATIONAL YOUTH DIRECTOR OF THE NAACP/JOURNALIST WITH BET

# PROLOGUE

THREE MASKED MEN PASS ON THE PASSENGER'S SIDE BEFORE turning and shooting through the back window.

Tat! Tat! Tat! Tat! Tat!

Dough's hit in the head repeatedly. He's slumped in the driver's seat gasping for air; the passenger suffers minor injuries. Blood's pouring from Dough's dreadlocks, down his face. Discombobulated and in pain, he's flashing back on his life of crime. He thinks about his infant baby girl as she's seconds away from being fatherless. He can't move . . . he can't see . . . he can't breathe . . . He realizes what he's getting ready to leave behind. Blood swallows his face like sweat in the Sahara Desert.

Rotating 360 degrees clockwise, I become light-headed and my stomach wants out.

"*Where the fuck am I!* I think trying to decode my darkened location. Why am I strapped upside down to a wooden frame spinning? Why are there strange masked men standing before me? As I turn my head to the side as much as the restraining rope will allow, getting a better look at what's pinning me down, it dawns on me. I am a dartboard for what appears to be a game played by four or five covered accomplices. Spinning around, stunned to realize darts weren't being thrown, as the substitute, I make for excellent target practice as shot after shot seeps through my fleshy tissue.

Boom. The first shot is faultless. It tears through my T-shirt altering its color to a highlighted red. As the next shot follows, Boom, I try shunning the deadly slugs meant to take my life but am unable to. Wiggling, and squirming, I am immobilized and therefore have to welcome the next slug like accepting death in life.

At this stage, my head is numb; I go into a serene stupor. My thoughts muse on past endeavors of me putting it down on fools. Instead of sorrow and remorse after a successful strike, I triumph in stacking and B-hopping, applauding myself for my labors. My cause for violence demonstrates my deadly state of mind, for now I am a P.O.B., prisoner of bangin', as they gloat and tirade in uproar with each painful shot. I want to close my eyes and avoid witnessing my own demise.

Riding through the woods of South Mountain Reservation with five Bloods and one lone frightened Crip, we have a true feast. We set the Crip on fire. As he burns to death, the flames grow bigger in size from his flesh roasting like a turkey. His screams amplify along with my fulfillment. Watching the face of this Crip burn, my vision sharpens with a raised brow as I can see my own face in the flames. I watch my homees taunt me as I am the one burning.

Then my home girl Dakota is raped and beaten to death behind my building. When she's found, she has a sock lodged in her throat, eyes rolled back, and looks beyond deplorable. Revenge is all I have sought thereafter.

Scribbles, blares, and static send me to my homee Meggette, who is shot by a Blood. I can taste the smoke flaring from the gun used to shoot him in the back of the head six times. Seeing him on the ground motionless, drowning in his own Blood, thinking about all the life he has just abandoned, leaves me unresponsive. "Machete, Machete, help me, where are you, I'm dying!" he cries while I cradle him in my arms.

Mega Ru killed . . . Reggie burned . . . Ry-John suicide . . . Speedy killed . . . Dennis killed . . . Tray murdered . . . Bonnie killed . . . Boogie murdered . . . Slash killed . . . Sleepy killed . . . Kody murdered . . . Meggette killed . . . Dough murdered . . .

Right before the devastation of this next episode, I have an omen. My guardian angel should have whispered in my ear: Make right with your God while you can, friend, because all things must come to an end. Your number is next.

It's somewhere around 11:00 P.M. when I make a quick stop to the liquor store to cop some 40s. A stranger chauffeurs me around. The earth signs already reveal to me earlier that tonight is a night of death. Full moon, fools trippin', and me cherried up is the trio required for danger. However, when and where is unknown to me so my premonition is set aside as my soul seeks quenching.

Dressed down in red sweats accompanied by red Puma's with bright-ass red laces, I permit my wife-beater to reveal my physique.

Tattoos making a firm statement of my reputation, I walk with confidence.

Once inside, I scroll over a row of beers before eyeing up my counterpart, Olde mothafuckin' English. Heading to the counter with my goods, I hand the clerk a twenty-dollar bill.

Hearing the store's entrance bell sound, I make contact with male after male totaling five entering the store all seemingly dressed alike, orange baseball caps and blue Dickies pants. Making eye contact with the two in the front, I turn my attention back to the counter as the clerk rings up my brews. As one by one they pass me, I feel the cold electricity brush up against me, the pressure of their bodies sucking the life right out of me.

Hosting small talk, I turn my head to the side to exercise my peripheral, and low and behold, what do I find: enemies! Enemy, enemy, enemy, enemy, enemy; my heart pulses into an adrenaline rush post recognizing the opposing side. Mothafuckin' Hoover Crips. *Damn!* I think as I secretly feel my waist only to realize I am as naked as a newborn baby. *Damn, if I get out of this shit, I ain't neva goin' nowhere without my fuckin' strap again.* I can feel the eye fucking taking its course behind me as my attire states who and what my attachments are.

Every inner-felt defense tells me that something is about to pop. My heart thumps in my chest. I can smell the hate gyrating.

Oh, how I think these fools are gonna fade me on sight because I've been caught slippin'. A banger's payday and the other's pink slip. Turning around once again trying to decipher their intentions, I know they are on to me. *Fuck!* One of them I recognize from a previous shootout, typical shit—can't stop. Revenge is a mothafucka! I know vengeance is all he can think of as I try to figure out how to counter their offense.

"Eleven dollars is your change, sir, would you like a plastic bag to go with that?" Looking back at the clerk, I think, *Maybe he's got a strap behind the counter, but how the hell am I gonna get it?* With no patience for that plan, Plan B is leniency from my foes in my fatal error in getting caught out-of-bounds.

Not wanting to waste any more time, and trying to elude getting my toe tagged, I rudely respond, "Nah man, I'm good, just hurry up!" Eyeing up the clerk for some sense of support is useless, for he is a civilian and off-limits.

With me at the counter, and them behind me, I am defenseless. Accepting my change, I steal one more peek at the group before flat-lining toward the exit. Inches from the door, I feel the tension thicken, and the anxiety of being shot from behind. Hoping I won't be downsized by gunfire on the outside, I am showered with bullets from the inside.

Pop! Pop! Pop!

Call it instinct or second nature because I drop my beers instantly and take off. I'm cautious not to look back too soon because the first twenty feet of separation between them and me are the most critical. That is the severance needed to secure the best chances of a zigzag getaway.

Half a block away, I see people standing on their porches self-engulfed in their own worlds. Mumbling to the air around me, "Damn! What the fuck is goin on?"

I appear schizophrenic and on the loose. There is a pay phone along the way but there is no time to stop and make a call for backup. To my right is a truck; a man leans up against it with a sign that portrays an arrow directing me to continue along the path. A female stands to my left with a sign, "Hi, I'm Karma," while an arrow under directs me to make a left. Rounding the corner, I spot an alley that I figure I can easily escape into. With darkness in my support it adds to my nervousness. More shots follow me as this time my right ear is grazed. Hysteria grabs me by the throat. My lungs are burning. In shock, reaching for my wounded ear, Blood spurting down my face, getting away seems further and further away. "Agghh shit! I'm hit! Mothafucka!" Turning back to size up my distance from the enemy, I realize they are nowhere in sight, which is comforting for a second, but shots continuously pass me, stealing my hope. Nonstop running and perfect textbook strides; I can't allow them to finish me this way for my escape is just a few feet away. *Where the fuck are they, where do I go, I can't get caught, I'm tired of running, what should I do?* Heart pounding, eyes on the prowl, mind racing, and feet hurting, I can't seem to escape gunfire.

Finally, spotting a semi-cracked garage door with a humongous X hovering on it, I maneuver my way under and lie still on the dust-ridden floor behind a pipeline that shields most of my body. Holding my breath and freezing all movements, my thoughts incite a deadly riot. *Who are they—nigga you know—what do they want—yo' life, where are they—coming for you—and why do they want me—Karma?*

*Oh shit!* Karma! That was the bitch who guided me in here. Her name isn't Karma; it's karma out to get me.

A couple minutes elapse as I think about ditching this garage, but realize I'd better just lay low for a moment.

*Should I get out, what if they are waiting for me, this is some bitch shit hiding in here, man the fuck up, hell no stay the fuck in here, maybe they left.* As the seconds wind down, life becomes dear to me.

Silhouettes of the enemy troops are visible in the short distance separating me from the entrance, plus I am not able to detect the number of soldiers after me.

As I watch for movement under the cracked area of the garage, all of a sudden things get quiet. *Maybe they've gone away.* Then I hear grunts, and as I look around, they are everywhere. They wait to see if I am going to make a move. The shadows of my foes welcome me with guns aiming and searching for my whereabouts.

"We know you in here slob, you don't wanna come out and play cuzzz?"

A herd of anxiety shoots through me, but my survival instincts silence me.

"Look!" one of them shouts in victory, pointing to me.

"We got him!"

*Fuck!* I sound off internally as my chest tightens, and body begins trembling uncontrollably. Terror seizing the pit of my stomach.

*I'm gonna die,* I think with painful clarity. *So this is how it ends . . .*

As they connect my location to the trickles of Blood left behind, I am grabbed by the forearm and dragged to the center of the garage, forcing me to look into my foes' nightly eyes. Some of them have pistols. Some wave knives at me, bats, even chain saws. I know I am going to be executed. *This is it.*

I'm repeatedly stomped on like first base, and punched like a bag. Minutes thereafter, they stop, leaving me to believe the worst has subsided. *Who are they and why are they so persistent in capturing me?*

Me on the ground, and them standing around me in a circle, I realize these people are not the fools from the liquor store; they are victims from past crimes. Two of them are women, and seven or eight Crips mixed in. One of the women stands out because she is a nurse Meggette and I robbed for over a G and some fine jewelry. *Where da five Crips from earlier?* These seven or eight, most of which I can't recollect except for their blue attire and gangster talk, all were victimized by me. I have no idea of the names of these people, their facial features, or their races.

As I roll over next to a table, I slowly scan each and every one of their faces. Guns and knives are now visible and waiting to enter me. I question my anger for them considering we are cut from the same quality of breed, but accepting me on the losing end isn't idyllic.

As the first shot is fired, my forearm shields my face from taking the hit. Agghh! I scream but the pain upon impact isn't as bad as I would have expected. Two more shots follow in quick succession, now puncturing flesh in my torso, sending Blood squirting five feet ahead of me. "Agghh! Agghh! Yo, what da fuck!" Like the first shot, though, minimal pain but by far more effective this time as I spew out globs of Blood. Starring up at barrels and faces of laughs and snickers, I channel up all the strength left in me to mount some kind of attack. Shuddering on my feet, I move to the side and back up against a table.

I have no idea where to go or what to do.

I'm soaked with Blood from head to toe, leaving a puddle where I stand. I force my hands into fighting position, swinging them recklessly, but I don't have the energy to hold my balance, then another shot lands to my skull sending me crashing through the table.

With dizziness, and much more pain this time, Blood oozes down my face as I lie on the pavement in complete terror. Now my enemy is finally going to put me to rest. I drift in and out of consciousness. Grabbing my head to compress the hole, Blood suffuses my face. Revenge has come in its most prolific form, total obliteration. They are disposing of me as dispassionately as they captured me. When I change positions, I feel icy currents of Blood gyrating in my head to whatever side I lean to.

All standing over me, they begin to open fire in cadence while shouting at me, "Die mothafucka, die! Die! Die mothafucka!"

I throw my arms around my head and curl up in the fetal position. Shots come from every direction jerking my hole-ridden body from side to side. More cheers, exuberant laughter, and victory slurs play over and over in my head, "Die mothafucka, die!"

But I still can't feel the amount of pain comparable to the devastation caused. As the moments get darker, suddenly I start to deflate as I slowly begin feeling sleepy. The world spins rapidly.

This is the end. Mental pictures of my life parade before my eyes. Snapshots of my childhood are revealed to me. I hear simultaneously music in the far distance. Something like jazz or a fine-tuned classical piece. My stomach lurches.

Faces drift through my mind too. I make out living relatives, Mom, daughter, and brothers.

I am never going to see them again.

*I don't wanna die like this. My family needs me. Who's going to give Da-Shana away at her wedding? I want to be at her high school and college graduation. Who's going to teach her about boys?*

And then my dead homees mesh into my thoughts simultaneously: Meggette, Tray, Mega, Dough, Dakota, Rel, Denise, Boogie, Sleepy, Speedy, and Slash . . .

Trying to muster up enough willpower not to lose consciousness, I continue to fight as I keep digesting slugs.

Boc, Boc, Boc, Boc, Boc, Boc, Boc, Boc, Boc.

While my eyelids begin to give way, still fighting to hold on, still consuming bullets, I decide I can't hold on any longer. They win and I lose. With consciousness now forsaking me, I prepare myself to head home. Darkness envelops me. Deep, complete.


"Let me the fuck go!"

Whack! "Shut the fuck up slob!"

Watching these Crips hold my little baby girl down demolishes every living cell, purity, and sanity inside me.

Closing my eyes asking, *God, please, don't let them do this.*

"God can't help you now mothafucka." Whack!

My screams and yells are so thunderous and violent, my cries full of rage and terror, Blood shoots through my eyes. Everything in my vision turns from clear and common to red and Bloody. *How perverted, she's just a baby,* I think.

"Don't do this, it's me you want, leave her alone. Please! Please! Don't do this!" Watching them fondle, hit, and impersonate her innocent howls increases my madness to insanity. I can't do shit to protect my princess. I yank, jerk, and tug with all the force and strength the Lord has given me. I rip through the flesh around my wrist leaving the rope restraining just my bone. My ankles are shackled and weakened from the nails jolted through them. I bellow endlessly, so loud, so long, that I throw up my Adam's apple. Then my baby girl looks at me, "Daaadddddy!" What a blissful exclamation, but a father's worst nightmare under this condition. As she cries, I cry begging for the strength to break free and slaughter these fuckers.

I search deep within for a plan or an ingenious idea. But nothing; just visible torture.

With no way to break free, I watch on suffering the humiliation until I deflate. Tears start running, uncontrollably, down my face. Looking on through a blurred vision my spirit is finally broken.

My failure to rescue her is a timeless wait for execution. At the point where I think I can't take any more, the point of absolute mortification, I dart up to the foot of my bed sweating like a slave.

"Dae! Dae! Dae! Dae! Dae!" while shaking me vigorously. "It's aright! It's fine! It's just a dream! It's okay!" Neina whispers. Awaking to her concerned tone is insurance that I am still living. Her alarmed presence reassures me that I am having another episode, or should I say *nightmare*. Turning toward her as she patiently waits for me to regain my senses so she can console me, her facial vibes speak volumes.

"Are you okay, Dae?" Bearing in mind past attempts to tranquilize me in these terrifying conditions, and the blows that followed, she hesitantly embraces me with her right arm while cupping my face with the other. Now, under the charm of her touch, I gradually descend from a hard-nosed rant and rave to a slow wail. Without her voice and hands to bring me back, I would have been pushed out of my existence. As she wipes my moistened face, I search for any leftover manliness.

Before losing myself in a deleterious horrifying sleep just a few hours ago, death locked itself in my mind and discarded the key. I was obsessing, rollin' around in my brain death and all that accompanied it, rigor mortis, maggots, coffins, and tears. I was in full-throttle dismemberment thinking about the afterlife.

Juggling between the flashes of devastation I've caused, now to be on the receiving end of shots fired and flesh punctured, I am now forced to accept my past as a reality.

# THE BEGINNING OF AN END

*A plant with dreams to be a tree*
*Placed in a garden*
*A garden unlike the garden of his birth*
*Bitter with the taste of impure water*
*For the garden was poison*
*Bitter water for the times*
*Now is later to become oh so sweet*
*Victory was not the plant's sweet taste*
*Defeated before the start of his growth*
*These marked the signs of the plant's beginning*
*The start of my ending*

DEATH AND TURMOIL ARE HOT ON MY HEELS. THEY PURSUE me with relentless passion. In their anger and contempt, they torture me—body and soul—beating me, wounding me, and robbing me of my ability to value life—my own or any other. In the darkness of the streets, my childhood is murdered; innocence is shot. Yet, in the dawn of a new nightmare I am resurrected with earned power and respect. I am reborn—a gangster.

• • •

It's summer, 1990, and without forewarning, my younger brother, Derrick, and I are ordered to pack up and head out by Mama. We are moving across country from New Jersey to Phoenix—a long way from home, friends, and our mother. I am nine years old and leaving her behind.

Those who have been to Phoenix, or the P-zone as we call it, can relate to my experiences there. If asked before moving to Phoenix of my opinion of its natives, my answer would have been that they are a bunch of funny-talking country bumpkins compared to the fast-talking city slickers back east.

My uncle flies to my aunt Claudette's house in Irvington, New Jersey, just to drive my brother and me to Phoenix. My mother isn't taking the trip with us; she'll fly to Phoenix in the weeks to come. My older brother, David, is already there. Our journey cross-country lasts four days.

Every summer my relatives Abdul, Irshad, Quadir, and Samad visit us in Jersey. This year will be their last; we're going back with them for good. The carpool consists of six kids, with Irshad and me being the oldest of the bunch.

Uncle prepares himself for the drive by making one last prayer. Inside the house, I am getting my last hug from Mama. Uncle is down on all-fours. His forehead is touching the ground. *What's he doing?*

Our trip takes us through many states, but none longer than Texas. Everything is so different I feel like I'm traveling through a foreign country. The air is so hot and the humidity so thick it's like trying to breathe through cotton stuffed up your nose. There are weird-looking trees and birds I've never seen before. I'm completely out of my element. The only knowledge I have of mountains, deserts, and cactus comes from what I've seen on television when I used to watch old Western movies at my stepfather's house.

We finally arrive in Phoenix. The air is even thicker and

heavier than Texas. The trees catch me by surprise. I thought trees like these could only be found on islands. And the streets are in better condition than the potholed roads in Jersey.

Derrick and I move to Aunt Sabrina's house on East Chipman Road between 18th and 19th Streets in Park South Phoenix. The house is crammed. My two older relatives, Belinda and Athena, share a room. In my room, I sleep on the bottom bunk with my older brother, David. On the top are Irshad, Derrick, and Abdul. It's not the most comfortable setup and being separated from my mother makes me unable to relax in this new environment.

A few days later, I receive a phone call from Mama.

"Hey Mommy! Mom, when are you coming? I miss you!"

"Soon baby. I'll be there before you know it. So do you like it down there?"

"I dunno. I wanna come back home, Mommy. Why we gotta all sleep in the same room?"

"Who's in the room with you baby?"

"Mom there's no room. I have to sleep in the bed with David and he always pushes me out."

"Listen baby, please be patient, you gon' have to make do for now. It's all we have right now so tough it out for a few more weeks. Things'll change when I get there, I promise. Okay?"

"Yeah Mommy."

"Let me speak to your brother, I love you—you hear me?"

"I love you too Mommy."


Park South covers an area from 16th to 24th Streets bounded by Baseline, Broadway, and Roeser Roads. Buckeye Road—24th Street and 24th Avenue—is home to the majority of the city's Black population. It also is the 'hood of Phoenix's most hostile street gangs—both Bloods and Crips. Hispanic neighborhoods are between Greenway and Bell Roads and 32nd Street and Cave Creek Road. Fifteenth Avenue, 23rd Avenue, Southern Avenue, and Broadway Road belonged to the Lindo Park Crips.

My aunt's house has three bedrooms with four closets. The kitchen counters are tile with specks of Black. There's a stone fireplace with an exposed stone chimney in the living room and a beautiful beamed ceiling. Behind the house is a spacious yard. It's ideal to have BBQs and take full advantage of the Western atmosphere. The front lawn is gigantic with a palm tree in the front that provides remarkable shade in the summer.

Just as I feared, things change in weird ways within days of us moving in. Already, I begin feeling lonely with the absence of my mother. *Why did Mommy send us here? Maybe she don't want us no mo'.* I know I'm not the best kid, but what did I do for us to get shipped out? *Why didn't she send me to my father's house?*

Oblivious to the fact that my aunt, uncle, and all my relatives I now live with are Muslim, I have to dramatically change my life. I don't even know what Muslims are let alone how to live as one. They wear these funny outfits, with caps on their heads. Prayer controls their lives because they pray all day.

I thought people only prayed before eating dinner. Back home, I had the luxury of doing what I wanted, going to bed when I wanted, eating what I wanted, and celebrating Christmas and Halloween. Back home I was a wild child, undisciplined, and free from adult supervision. All the things I'm not allowed to do now that I'm under my aunt's supervision merely went unnoticed by my mama in Jersey.

Here, pork is forbidden, and you can forget about seconds at dinner. Rated-R programs are restricted and bedtimes imposed. I never realized the luxuries I had until I was deprived of those very same things.

My aunt Sabrina is a fourth-grade teacher so she believes in year-round schooling. Cs and Ds are not acceptable and she possesses patience to a T as she tutors us on our weakest subjects.

I hate the house rules because everything here is so systematic and I'm not used to all this routine. There's a chart for who'll wash the dishes, who'll take out the garbage, who'll set the table, and even what we'll eat for the entire week.

I wallow in homesickness much of the time. Throughout my stay, my asthma is aggravated by the atmosphere and stifling heat. Sometimes I have to struggle to breathe in the air, which makes my asthma pump sacred.

Unhappy as I am, my stay does have its benefits. The scenery, for one thing, is dope. Across the street from the house looms a stunning yard with colorful flowers and statues. This is a profound contrast to Jersey's poverty-abandoned buildings, pimps, bums, fiends, and junkies. In Phoenix, I don't have to worry about the ghetto landscape of gutter rats, possums, and man-eating cockroaches. Here, there's room to enjoy simple things.

During the summer, I experience new things: water fights, chasing snakes, scorpions, lizards, and horny toads. I've never seen a lizard before, let alone a scorpion. My relatives are comfortable being hands-on with these creatures. In addition, I'm welcomed by my first fierce sandstorm. While everyone else goes into prerehearsed maneuvers, I'm left to feel the wrath. I learn that the storms can hit without warning, and other times you can tell one is coming by the knots of dust devils discoing their way across the wasteland. Once the wind grabs the sand, you can only see a few inches ahead of your face. If you can't find a car or side of a house to take cover when the storm ripens, you best cower down and shut your mouth and eyes.

Adjusting to the Muslim way of life is a whole new challenge and makes me feel like I'm living in someone else's world. Aunt Sabrina is devoted and completely addicted to her religion, allowing no room for clemency in our gradual conversion. I feel imprisoned. Going from an unrestricted lifestyle to an absolute dictatorship is culture shock.

My aunt is a medium-built woman with a coffee skin tone. She wears blossoming house dresses and sandals. She's strict, religious to the bone, but at times has a wonderful sense of humor.

My uncle signs me up for his Pop Warner football team. He has a full beard that he always combs, and a bald head that makes him look scary. His dark brown eyes see only two possibilities for doing things, his way and the wrong way. His deep, threatening voice commands your attention, and he is adamant about discipline. His face projects a weathered ghetto roughness, yet he looks youthful when he smiles. His facial expression hardly ever changes as he wears a mask of proud distress.

During my first day of football practice, I'm approached as I cross the field.

"Where you from home-bwoy?" a boy taller than me asks. He has on a red shirt and a red pair of Jeepers, which is what they called Chuck Taylors. He speaks with a funny accent.

"New Jerzey." I hold his stare.

"Say what! What set chu from fool?"

Ignorant to his question, I ask him, with a puzzled expression, "What . . . what I'm from?"

He looks at me like I'm crazy and even laughs.

"What street chu' live on?"

Trying to get hold of the conversation, he makes a weird barking noise as four other boys close in on me. I don't turn. My chest tightens.

"Who you down wit'? Who put you on the set?" demands a shorter boy. *Is this a challenge?* I feel they are interrogating me, waiting for the wrong answer. I don't know the right one. My heart begins to pound and my mouth gets dry.

I fight off their confusion with an aggressive response. "What set I'm from?"

"Hey Blood," the shorter one says to the taller boy. "I think that's the nu kid from Nu Joisey, Coach's son. Remember he was telling us his son was moving down here and was going to play on the team?"

Sensing some hope, I support their notion. "No no no, he's my uncle."

"Wass yo' name?"

"Dashaun."

A puzzled look passes their faces simultaneously. "That's what they call you?"

Confused by his concern, I mumble "yeah."

"Homee awright," one of the boys adds. "Listen homee, around here there's a lot of gangs. Y'all don't have gangs in Nu Joisey?"

*Gangs, what are you talkin' about?*

"Nah."

"You gotta be careful where you go and what you wear."

I'm dumbfounded at what he tells me because in Jersey, my friends call themselves GST, Grove Street.

*Is that a gang?*

For the next twenty minutes, I listen on like an employee in training. *Huh? What? Why can't you wear that? Crabs . . . blue . . . shoelaces . . . belts . . . flags. This is crazy.* The taller boy explains how Bloods and Crips operate. That everything is geographical. Crossing the wrong boundaries can cost you your life. He goes into what the colors mean, *red, green, Black, blue, orange, gray, brown,* and where not to wear them. He explains that hats, shoes, shoelaces, belts, barrettes, shirts, and flags tell which gang you're with. I learn the names of sets like West Side City Crips, Park South Killer Gangsta Bloods—7 Line, Vista Bloods, 79 Swans, and the Broadway Gangsters, and too many Mexican gangs.

The more he talks the more complicated gangs become to me. *How can colors stop me from going where I wanna?*

A coach's whistle chimes in, momentarily distracting our attention. As the crowd around me begins to disperse, the first boy remains and extends his hand. "I'm Baby Maniak from da Hilltop Bloods." He's friendlier now. When we lock palms, he forces my hand into an awkward grip locking both of our index and thumb fingers together. *What the hell was that?*

"You need to talk to the set where you live so they can teach you."

Baby Maniak is the first Blood I meet.

In my aunt's neighborhood, males and females wear red or blue shirts, pants, shoes, shoelaces, bandannas, belts, underwear, socks, jackets, and barrettes on their heads. So now, it all makes sense to me why everyone wears these colors, they are BLOODIN' and CRIPPIN'.

While shooting hoops with Irshad, a boy with a red shirt enters our yard. Irshad introduces me to Ammo as his relative from Nu Joisey.

"Wezzz up homee?"

I shoot back with a grin on my face, "Wassup."

Ammo lives at the end of the block.

Ammo is the type of kid that needs little instigation to beat you up. He's respected on the block by virtue of his older brother, Mean D. He speaks with a heavy accent that often leaves me clueless after he finishes his sentence. His dress style is unique, militant, all sharp creases and solid colors.

My friendship with Ammo soon accelerates my acceptance with the other boys in the neighborhood. Ammo is the biggest ten-year-old I've ever seen.

•  •  •

I spend the next few months adjusting to Phoenix life and culture.

Third grade starts off rocky for me as I endure a few tests. One of many stands out as a worthwhile lesson. In my class, the majority of students are Mexican, followed by a solid force of Blacks.

In the seat next to mine there's a Mexican boy named Ivan who weighs more than I do. For some unknown reason, my ways are insulting to him. It isn't long before, disgruntled with me simply speaking, he advances to open threats.

One morning during class, he whips out a slingshot and aims it directly at me. I leap to safety behind my desk as a rock strikes the other side with a thump. *What is he doing? What did I do to him?*

What bothers Ivan about me, I think, is not only the implied insult of my untraditional East Coast style, but the fact that I won't acknowledge myself as inferior to him. His posse laughs at all his corny jokes, and puts him on a pedestal. Not me.

Later that day, he makes it a point to sit next to me at lunch, so he can further instigate me. Throughout the meal he criticizes my appearance and the way I speak. "You can't sit at this table homez; you talk like a nerd, all proper." His friends join in the laughter. I pay no attention to them, although inside I feel humiliated. I know I need a comeback but the fear and embarrassment paralyze me.

Finally he threatens, "Boy, I'm a get chu homez!" I am sure he means it.

"I'm a beat chu down punk. Wassup now homez!"

At last, I choose to confront the matter with all the toughness I can muster. "Why you keep messing with me?" I ask.

"Say what? I ain't gotta explain nothing to you punk." At this point, his camp tosses in a few "Ohh's," hyping the situation to guarantee a fight. Wasting no time, my decision is made. I rip into Ivan with all my might, trying to punch his lights out. Gaining leverage and throwing him up against the Blackboard, I connect a jaw-shaking jab after jab to his face nonstop until his three comrades jump in and begin beating me with uncontrollable rage.

"Stooop! Stop! Get off! Stooop!" I shout.

Ivan, panting like a dog, makes them take turns kicking me. I focus on tightening my muscles to minimize the pain of the kicks. As other students cheerfully pack around in a circle cheering them on, I hear a whistle from outside the class. Like trained warriors in a prizefight, they unthinkingly stop ratpacking me and separate.

Ivan and his circle run from the classroom and scatter down the hall, shouting obscenities along the way, promising retribution. Wiping specks of Blood from my mouth and straightening my clothes, I feel humiliated and weak. Although I'm content with my performance until his homees assisted him, the feeling of being a victim hurts.

I want to tell Ammo what happened, but I can't. *They gon' think I'm weak; I'm a punk if I tell them I got beat up. They gon' tease me.* I keep my rumble to myself.

After this altercation, I realize that surviving in Phoenix means I need my own homees to have my back. Out here on my own, I'm not safe. I don't have much choice; I'm surrounded by gangs and all my friends are down with them.

Hanging out with Ammo, I learn a lot in a few months. Still feeling like an import, I long for acceptance. Mama's absence increases my participation with the gang. I don't feel comfortable hanging around them, but I can't stand being in the house, and I know protection is needed.

*Where is she? She lied to me. She ain't coming. I'm a have to live here forever. I don't care if they tease me today. I don't care what they think about me. Anything is better than staying in that house. I'm tired of cleaning. Sick of doing dishes. I hate being told what to do and get-*

*ting whipped with switches. I can't take it anymore. Why does Mama even let Auntie hit me? She ain't my mother. Uncle ain't my father. He don't even like me. I need you, Mama. Where are you?*

Days pass by before I hear from Mama again. Receiving the phone from Auntie, I sit at the table.

"How are you baby?" *What do you care?*

"Are you coming now? You told me you were coming a long time ago. When you coming?"

"I know. Mommy is sorry. I wish I could be there. I'm trying. I miss y'all boys. How are y'all doing?"

I shrug one shoulder, wiping away built-up tears.

I mutter, "I don't wanna stay here."

Looking around to make sure the coast is clear; I press the phone closer to my face.

"Mama, Auntie hit me with a stick. Uncle choked me for something I didn't even do. Abdul spilled milk on the floor and . . . Uncle thought I did it. I told him I didn't do it but he still grabbed my neck. When are you coming? I don't want to live here."

I wipe my tears a second time, careful not to let Auntie hear me crying.

"Just try to stay out of his way. You know how your uncle is. I will be there soon baby, and you won't have to worry about that no more. I'll talk to Auntie about it, okay? I promise you baby, I will be there real soon. Just be a little patient. Let me speak to your brother. I love you." And just like that, we are disconnected again.

Living with my aunt and uncle, I am completely miserable. Every day it becomes harder to deal with being in the house and my spirit is regularly beaten down. Missing my mother and feeling like I have no family, my sadness makes me wonder if I'm worthy of being loved at all.

Most days, to avoid whatever is going on in the house, I force myself to join the neighborhood kids, catching the football, or chasing each other through alleys playing tag. Alleys stretch for blocks at a time, filled with graffiti-written walls sprayed with *"BLOOD ZONE—Bware."* My adjustment to the gang is slow and I still don't quite fit in. But if I want to have any sense of family and brothers who are down for me, I have to make this work. At times I want to lock myself within a padded room because of the fear I feel when I'm around them. To Ammo, I'm cool, but the other boys treat me like an outcast.

A few weeks turns into months. No Mama. She still hasn't come. Her arrival is slowly fading from my expectations. Every time we speak, it's the same ol' story. *I'll be there real soon. I promise. Mommy got a few more things to take care of here, and then I'll be there.* I realize she's not coming. In the meantime, my coping mechanism is to suppress my feelings. I concentrate on fitting in with the gang, changing my outward personality to what is respectable on the streets, and hiding parts of the real me deeper within myself.

Then, during mid-December, out of nowhere, Mama appears. Despite my resentment, I'm glad to see her. I want to tell her about my feelings, but I don't know how. I'm not the same little boy she sent away months ago; this place is changing me.

Nearing Christmas, I anticipate my yearly pleasure. A Christmas tree, toys, maybe a bike, or a remote control car, candy canes, and colorful lights. It's what I wait for all year. Talking to Mama shortly before the big day, I'm hit with a bombshell.

"Dashaun, Auntie being Muslim means she doesn't celebrate Christmas."

"So what does that gotta do wit' us? I'm not getting no toys this year, Mama?"

It's Christmas Eve and I'm beside myself with disappointment. Christmas is my favorite holiday. I count down the days until I can dash into the living room and open my gifts. It's not the myth I'm hypnotized by, but the attention. Christmas is the time I feel most important. In my mama's house, classical Christmas music can be heard everywhere from morning to night. All my relatives enjoy the festivities of gift giving at my uncle Pooch's house. Oh, how I wish I could feast on some of the traditional food: pork, rice, chicken, and sweet potatoes.

However, this Christmas Eve things are different.

When morning arrives Derrick and I race into the living room only to be welcomed by Uncle praying. *No tree, no presents, no music. I know this gotta be some kind of joke.* Looking at Mama on the couch asleep, I begin to fume. *See Ma. See what you did! Why did we have to come here?*

Sensing Christmas is lost forever, I add another chip on my shoulder.

Weeks later, a mob of us are playing football in the street, something we love to do. What starts out as a clean, touch-only game can, as the competition intensifies, change into an all-out tackling match. On this day, Ammo catches a pass when BJ blindsides him. Adding insult to injury, BJ then boasts about the big hit like he made the top ten on ESPN's *SportsCenter*.

"Yeah! Yeah! Don't come 'cross tha middle again."

Lying on the ground, unable to move, Ammo looks up at our faces.

Getting to his feet, full of pain and embarrassment, Ammo curses at BJ. He's irritated because BJ won't back down.

"Why you hit me like dat! It's just a game, buster!"

However, to everyone's surprise, BJ matches Ammo's aggressiveness and charges him with a push to the chest sending him flying backward to the ground again. Everyone looks at each other, thinking, *Oh shit, he done messed up.* When Ammo stands, he takes off running down the block toward his house while BJ continues taunting.

"You know his brother gon' come out here," someone says.

"Fuck Mean D, I got brothers too." Mean D is cliqued up with the Vistas and he's always with a crowd of his young Bloods. BJ lives on Roeser, which is four blocks away; I don't know where his brothers' house is. Not that it matters because his brothers can't help him now. Mean D makes his way down the block in a slow B-Dawg swagger, body fully decorated with tats, and a red belt with the buckle turned to the back. Behind him, Ammo shadows his every step as do three of his soldiers. Everybody knows Mean D isn't one to fuck with, as he totes guns on a regular basis and has an entourage of riders. When there's gunfire on or around Chipman, best believe Mean D's behind it.

"On Blood, who'da fuck faded my li'l brother Blood?"

I feel ill inside at the sound of the word Blood coming from his mouth.

Knowing BJ's responsible, all eyes turn to him. I figure at this point BJ is going to haul ass, but his posture and answer suggest differently. While standing firm in his position, his voice is squeaky and unsure. "W-w-we was just playing football, an-and I tackled him."

Mean D responds in a grimy tone, "Nah mothafucka, fuck dat," Mean D clearly vexed. "You try'n fade my brother, nigga? Wass happ'nin' Blood?"

Before BJ can answer, Mean D socks him with two blows to the face. Ammo retrieves a mini Louisville Slugger from the back of his pants and repeatedly whacks BJ. *Oh my God, stop hitting him, won't somebody help him!* At some point, BJ gives up trying to fight back and takes an ass whipping he'll never forget. Everyone's laughing loudly, so I join, but inside I'm crying and my legs and hands are trembling. I'm scared for BJ. I want to run away from what I see, but can't. My feet feel stuck in the cement. I am nauseated, and my head is spinning.

*What's so funny? Are y'all crazy?* I want to help BJ but I'm not getting my ass beat. As BJ lies helpless on the concrete, Mean D begins choking him seconds away from his death. I see BJ's eyes; they are lifeless. He's barely moving. I want to cry. That sick feeling enters my stomach. At this point, the tallest of his three comrades grabs Mean D, saving BJ's life. BJ struggles to sit up but can't. He clutches his neck with one hand, his head with the other. His face is beaten to the point of being unrecognizable. Ammo stands over him, just out of kicking range, and spits in his face, a gooey chunk that lands in his eye. He then does a weird-looking dance in celebration of his actions. *Why are they doing that to him?* My heart thumps out of control in my chest. *I'm glad it ain't me.* BJ is beaten, bruised, eyes swollen, teeth missing, and hair caked with his own Blood. Blood is coming out of his ears.

This experience shows me the power of the streets, the power of violence, and more important, the respect received from this type of power.

I gain a higher level of respect for Ammo. I admire the power he has. *I wish my older brother would do something like that for me.* What better form of love can a brother show than for his little brothers' safety? Defending your honor? My older brother, David, doesn't even acknowledge me. He comes and goes without so much as a ruffle of my hair.

Looking at BJ all Bloody and battered strikes a nerve in me. *Is this real?* What can cause somebody to hurt someone like this? Afterward, I make sure not to speak to Mean D. I don't want to say anything wrong and get the backlash of his anger. Violence equals respect while the weak get trampled. My goal is to fall in line with the former.

At night, when I finally manage to drift off, I dream that I'm being bludgeoned and people just watch. The next morning, I hesitantly feel my body for any bruises. I become afraid, since I can't tell the difference between nightmares and reality.

When we play manhunt, my speed is too much for the rest. The players include Ammo, Baby B, Li'l Twist, and Li'l Cyko. Baby B has a Jheri curl and deep pockets 'cause his parents have money. He always has paper on him and is always fly, rockin' the freshest fashions. Li'l Twist is adopted. I find this out when I see his parents, who are Latino. Li'l Cyko wears his hair in braids and is a rebel, completely out of line. He's wild, always fighting and getting suspended from school. With a slight breeze in the air, the weather is just perfect to make the game better. I have on a red and white shirt with tan khakis. Eluding Ammo, Baby B, and Li'l Cyko, I decide to expand my perimeter to suit the game. I run three blocks, sprint down the alley, hop a fence, and end up on Roeser Road. As Ammo shouts for me to come back, I foolishly run further into enemy territory.

"Wassup wit' you cuz!" an elder demands as he grabs me by the collar.

"Fucc you doin' round here li'l nicca?" one of his homees cuts in.

I'm terrified. Completely shook, I have no response. Tears stream down my face. *What I do?* With a blue flag around the face of my violator, I know what I've done. I've crossed the color line.

Two more Crips approach, and now they circle around me. Nowhere to run.

"How old iz you cuz?" He removes his flag covering his mouth.

Looking up into his eyes, I search for the words. Wiping my face I whisper, "Ten."

Seeing a gang of Crips spread out on the block dressed down in blue swells my fear. I'm shoved to the ground.

Looking at each other for what I assume is confirmation, one Crip says, "Stall cuz out. Li'l nicca ain't triccin'." With that, Ammo and B now aiding me, I feel safer with them here.

"Don't come 'round here no mo' cuz!" a Crip yells.

We turn and dart off. "West Side Crip Gang!" followed by a loud whistle followed by numerous chirps' echoes in the distance.

Back on Chipman, my tears will not stop. A small meeting is held on the sidewalk in the blazing sun. We're sopped in sweat. Now irritated, they look to vent their anger.

Baby B turns to me, eyes wide. "You can't do that. You can't bring that shit up here."

Ammo chimes in. "We don't go over there. If my brother finds out, he's gonna sock me out. Man . . . you can't do that again."

I wipe my face again. They're right; my guilt silences me. *How can I defend myself when I'm wrong? I'm always wrong.* They warned me before about going on Roeser, but all the excitement from the game blinded me. Names like Big C from West Side refresh my memory. The neighborhood talks about him a lot; how he's the one who lays Bloods down. He's the shot-caller and a major enemy of the Bloods. Because of his reputation history, he's both a legend and a major target. Standing there, inches from Ammo's face, I'm disappointed in myself. *That was close. At least we got away.* All these rules, colors, and sets still confuse me.

Twenty minutes later, Ammo, Baby B, Li'l Twist, Li'l Cyko, and Baby Gee lead me to the alley behind Chipman. They show me a wall with names spray-painted on it. *Who are they?*

"See these names?" Ammo points to the wall. "They are all

dead. Some of them was our ages too. My brother says you don't wanna get put on the wall."

I take a few steps back and compress my eyes. *BG, Tears, C-Slash, Li'l Munk, Big Fang, Baby Bone, Play Boy, Sal, Packman, Li'l Packman, Killa, Peaches, Al, Big T, and Dre.* My eyes scroll the wall in shock. *This ain't no game.* Looking around I see Baby Gee teary-eyed. *Damn, why is he crying, he acts like that's his mom or something. Is the wall personal to him? I don't want to be on that wall.* My lack of knowledge doesn't make me exempt from my obligation. My membership means competence. *I gotta get my shit together.*

Not long after, I'm scrutinized again. Walking to the corner store, we all count our change. The store is a converted house run by an elderly woman. In the living room, all bag and plastic items from potato chips to bread are displayed in a neat, organized fashion. A den off to the side has all pop items, from soda and juice, to water. The back den is a cornucopia of useless items like statues and figurines. In the front of the house, bam! Candy galore.

The owner is terribly thin and desiccated; her face has more wrinkles than a shirt at the bottom of a pile of laundry. After paying for an item, she motions for me to come closer to her while offering change. Unconcerned, I reach out and mid-transaction I feel her hand. I feel her bones under her skin as she croaks, "I'm old lady Chipper." While waiting for the rest of the gang, I take the liberty of quenching my thirst. As I tilt my quarter juice to my mouth, the gang begins to ridicule me.

"Agghh, Blood!" they shout with looming stares. "What chu doing? Don't drink dat!" another voice tag-teams. "Iz you brazy? I know you ain't puttin' dat poison in ya Blood homee." A few more taunts fly my way as I try to figure out why I'm the butt of mockery. As my eyebrows grow closer in confusion, theirs grow wider in surprise. In addition to the distance I see in their eyes, there's an awkward silence. I hold the juice up in front of my face to examine its contents.

"I can't drink this?" I feel like a child who just received an A and gets a beating for it. "Huhh!" More laughter comes as Li'l Cyko snatches my juice and tosses it in the trash can.

"Why you do that for?" I ask puzzled.

"We can't drink that kind'a juice. You gotta get the red one." My eyes flicker. I realize there is a thin line between our friendship and me crossing the line. I struggle to understand them. Inside, my body feels empty. My mind wrestles to make the connection. I feel weak and two steps behind.

Dealing with the gang is like walking on eggshells. Anything can be penalized. Just like in my house, there are rules and restrictions. I'm overwhelmed with the confinement in a free land. I make note to never drink blue juice again. Watching them exiting the store, I feel my status within the group plummet back to zero.

As time passes, graffiti makes itself more evident to me. I still can't understand most of it. I know the kids in the neighborhood write it, spray-painting every space visible, striking up the turf. My union with the neighborhood kids teaches me Bloods don't say or write words starting with c's. This is how Bloods disrespect Crips. They replace all c's with k's or b's and cross out all remaining c's in the word. My first assumption is that these people have spelling and speaking difficulties. They say car with a b, bar, or come here, bome here. I also learn what dissin' down means. Bloods call Crips Crabs or Rickets to disrespect them. Crips call Bloods Slobs or Snoops. I pick up on the dialect and dress code, and mimicking Ammo's gear helps me isolate my color preference: red.

However, I do find the footwear corny as hell because in Jersey, Nikes and Reeboks are the shoes of choice, not to mention the year-round Timberlands. But here, they wear Converse All-Stars.

In Jersey, if you wear Jeepers to school, you will be teased, and probably beat up if you aren't popular. Nikes are for the in crowd. Jeepers are considered poor people's shoes. As if we weren't all poor, Jeepers were beneath poor. In addition, here khaki pants or Levi's are perfect with plaid shirts. Only the top two buttons are buttoned, which leaves the remainder of the shirt open to expose the solid color shirt underneath. This is gang attire, dressed down. No matter how hot the weather, everyone still has on freshly creased khakis with long-sleeved plaids.

It's like a brotherhood among the young'stas in the neighborhood. Auntie and Uncle don't even notice me getting deeper into the gang, and wearing red.

Every morning when I leave the house, there they are, on the corner. It feels as though they are waiting for me. We all meet at the corner of Chipman and 18th, and joke on each other while walking.

After school, Ammo, Li'l Cyko, Baby B, and I meet up and start plotting our afternoon activities. Our homee Lazy is with us. This guy is a real character. We call him Lazy because his eyes are real low and for the fact that he's cheap. He can have a pocketful of money, but when we're all together trying to make a dollar out of our fifteen cents to get something from the store to share, he won't tell us he has money, and he won't chip in. So we all make pacts to finish missions from stealing apples out of a neighbor's yard, to stealing bikes from other blocks and shoplifting from old lady Chipper. She's at least seventy years old. It's damn near impossible for her to peep my swift hand movement from the box of candy to my pocket. While she assists one of us, someone else snatches a handful of candy. The gang teaches me this three months into my stay.

Our missions are very competitive. Every time someone completes one, rest assured bragging follows, which encourages another to pull off a craftier stunt. If someone steals a bike, I steal a better one. If someone hops in a yard and steals apples, I sneak around back and steal their laundry.

At age ten, I attend a few of the high school football games. I learn that, in Phoenix, the high schools are segregated by Bloods, Crips, and Mexican gangs. And the gangs are divided by the two main high schools. There's a gang war on the streets between South Mountain and Carl Hayden high schools. David and Belinda go to South Mountain, while Athena goes to Carl Hayden. After a game between the two rivals, the tension escalates. During this game, one side of the stadium is trued up wearing blue, and the other flamed up sporting red. During tackles on the field, brawls take place in the stands. These two teams despise each other. Gang signs are flashed every play throughout the game, along with nonstop taunts.

After the game, the fight jumps off on the field and parking lot. Hours later it moves close to my house, and I remember seeing over a hundred gang members, fighting like cats and dogs. I don't get involved but for some bizarre reason, I like it. The Phoenix Police Department interrupts the festival and the Bloods run westbound up Broadway. The Crips run east. Whoever is left gets cuffed to the paddy wagons. The violence excites me.

In the heart of my second year living in Phoenix, my attitude takes a spin for the worse and because of it, I'm often whipped. Not by Mama though, but by Auntie. *Why does Mama let her beat me?* I rebel against the house rules: breaking curfew, sneaking out, abandoning my chores, and cussing. I feel invisible inside a house full of people, all engrossed in their own lives. My mood swings aren't pronounced enough for anyone to notice?

In Auntie's house, there's a lot of emphasis put on the dinner table. We all have to help prepare institutional-sized dinners where everybody lines up with a plate and scoops their portions.

Not only did you have to eat all of your food, but taking too long will land a switch to your ass.

Auntie will send me into the backyard to retrieve a switch off the tree. I have to remove the leaves and branches myself before handing it over to her. I often try to choose the smallest switch I can find, but will be sent back into the yard to get a bigger one.

In the living room, Auntie waits for me.

Mama sits on the couch and I sense some hope. I search deep in Mama's eyes for security, interference, and protection. Before lying over the couch with my pants down, staring at Mama, the tears materialize before the whipping begins.

"Mama, please, I'm sorry, don't let—"

Swackk!

I cover my butt and legs with my hands, but Auntie keeps beating me. Mama sees and hears me crying and screaming. She watches as though my pain has nothing to do with her. When Auntie is tired, she stops. Resentment rages through me. I limp into the bedroom to care for myself, as no one else seems interested. I never understand why Mama never saves me.

Living in Phoenix changes me tenfold. Misery loves company. I begin to enjoy the drama of classmates getting beat up, teased, and seeing their money, pencils, book bags, hats, and pride taken. I get a sick thrill out of torturing animals, cussing, and rebelling. My toughness even shoots up a notch hanging around Ammo and the gang. Wearing my red shirts gives me a sense of pride and acceptance—a feeling I'm missing at home.

In school, violence is becoming more common. During gym class, Hector stabs Javon in the neck over a pair of Chuck Taylors. They both have the same Black pair on but Hector's is clearly older, and in worse condition. Hector, wanting an upgrade in shoes, punches Javon in the face. They argue and tussle while classmates circle around them chanting "Fight! Fight! Fight!"

Hector has tattoos on his neck, hands, and arms. Hector is down with the M, Mexican Mafia. He moved to Phoenix from East L.A. I make my way inside the circle to witness the fight that Hector is noticeably losing. Hector pulls out a box cutter, and slices Javon below the ear. Everyone begins shouting, "He's bleeding. Somebody help him!" Javon is rushed to the nurse's office by the late-arriving gym teacher where they treat him until the paramedics arrive. I don't understand why Hector stabbed Javon over some sneaks but realize that in Phoenix, Chuck Ts are the equivalent of money in Jersey.

In 1992, I'm eleven and, at school, Tray is transferred into my class. Sitting behind me, his arrogance is vibrant. "Man why I gotta be in this stupid class with these busters?" Tray says.

"All right now, just settle down. I won't tolerate that," Ms. Robblie demands.

The next week in class, by way of assignment, I'm partnered up with Tray. We connect. We learn we both have an interest in comic books. We begin bringing comics to class to trade. Eventually, Tray and I become good friends. Tray's from 17th Street. He is dark-skinned with an eighties Jheri curl. He has six brothers who are all Bloods. Two of his brothers pick him up from school every day always dressed in red. Seventeenth Street goes by PSKGB-7 Line, which is Park South Killer Gangsta Bloods.

As the months pass, I start hanging at Tray's house after school. There, I see how the Sevens operate. What really intrigues me about Tray is his freedom at home. His father is a typical dead-beat, and his mom can be found getting served on the block. His older brothers take care of the house, and him. His house is a classic ghetto house party: loud music with pounding bass, blunt smoke thick in the air, drinks being passed freely, and wall-to-wall

Bloods. It is a daring lifestyle and projects an aura of glamour that I want.

The Sevens' idea of fun is getting drunk off beer and bragging about work put in. They shout Blood slang and connect their hands in duo and trio stacks. I find out Li'l Tray drinks, smokes cigarettes and marijuana. A few times Q-Tip offers me a hit but I refrain because I have a severe case of asthma, and most times being in the presence of smoke irritates my condition. However, it's on the Seven block that I take my first drink, Night Train to be exact.

Sitting in Tray's room we get ready to head outside. His room looks like a typhoon whipped through it. His room is struck up with X7 everywhere. Red flags nailed to the walls. Before we leave, he pulls a pair of tan khakis from underneath his mattress and steps into them.

"Tray, why you put cho pants under yo bed?" I assume he's hiding them.

"We gotta have sharp breases in our pants. So if you sleep on them at night they'll be brispy in da mornin', bee," pointing to the textbook creases.

"Why don't you iron them?"

"I dunno, this how my brothers do it, this how everybody do it."

On our way downstairs, we hear loud laughter in the basement. We eavesdrop on Tray's older brothers and homees, mindful to keep quiet so we don't get caught. "What dey doing? Can you see?" Tray asks.

"Shhh, wait a minute I can't see." Inching the door open some more I see 357s, rifles, and a sawed-off 12-gauge shotgun that looks as tall as me littered throughout the room. Picture after picture is being snapped of Soul and the enormous Gauge propped over his shoulder like prey after a successful kill. I can't help but desire to be down.

Leaning on the door, it makes a creaking sound.

"Get cho li'l ass outta here B, befo' I bank you," someone shouts from the group inside. I slam the door shut, pivot, and run back up the stairs with Tray behind me. Before reaching the top, we're called back into the room. Reluctant to go back, we head downstairs. I allow Tray to go in first. *I hope they're not mad at me.* Entering the room, I find a spot on the couch.

Whatever the Sevens are involved in seems cool. Every day consists of the same things: after school, click up on the block, drink 40s, and score some licks. I learn through their bragging sessions that licks are robberies.

Soul stands up and passes a gun around the room. "Check this out homee. Brand fuckin' new. No work on it. You know we gotta test it out." He proudly passes the loaded piece around the room. Captivated, each person takes turns stroking, and aiming it. A few even stick the pistol down their pants reenacting whipping it out on their enemies. When my turn comes, I cradle it while examining its features. I've never held a real gun before. It's striking. I visualize walking around the streets with it on my waist.

I feel that sense of power later on when Soul shows me how to shoot it. Handing me the gun, pointing it at the streetlight, I hold it tightly with two hands, close my eyes, and squeeze the trigger.

"Pop! Pop!"

I can't describe the exhilaration. Instantly, I understand why Tray's brothers are hooked on guns.

I spend days mimicking handshakes the Sevens do before engaging in conversation. This ritual is quick and intriguing. It's clear anyone not a part of this secret society doesn't matter.

Q-Tip approaches Tray and me as we sit on the porch. He has on red shorts with a red flag hangin' from his pocket. His underwear is made out of red bandannas. He sports red laces in his Black Chucks while dipping with a gangster mask on. Dipping is a Seven block in-house walk that all Sevens master. They arch their right shoulder back as far as it can go, which inflates their pecs, or breast if it's a home girl, and walk stiff as a board. The arched arm is viewed as the number 7 while the left arm hangs straight down by the waist side signifying a number 1. The right thumb hooks to the front of their pants where the pelvic bone is.

I admire the bond between Tray and his brothers. It reminds me of all the things I'm missing. My older brother, David, is wrapped up in his own life. If he loves me, he doesn't show it. Most young boys want to mimic their older brothers, hang out with them and talk about girls.

Tray became much more of a brother to me than David. While leaving a local store in the neighborhood, Tray and I talk about comics.

Out of nowhere, I hear a voice, "Way-Gang mothafucka, Crack!"

Tray gets mauled by a guy accompanied by two friends. The individual who punches Tray has big eyes and an attention-grabbing scar on his cheek.

This joker has to be all of six feet, 160 pounds, and possesses a manly build. He pounds on Tray, who's barely a hundred pounds soaking wet. His two homees position themselves around me so I can't run.

"What cha'll doing?" I say in a scared voice.

"Shut up li'l mothafucka."

I think twice about saying something, but the sight of Tray getting beaten up in front of me encourages me to be brave, act like a soldier and a friend. Bravery can only be determined when opportunity presents itself. With numbers, age, and size on their side, the other two hoodlums are looking on, fixing their eyes like watching a movie. I scamper past the two, but in mid-stride, *bang!* They pounce on me. As I roll around in agony, trying to regain the air that is knocked out of me, I'm snatched by the collar, and forced to stand. A solid kick to the chest knocks me back to the ground. Everything is spinning now as I receive another kick to the stomach. Forsaking me, they dive on Tray in unison.

I stagger to my feet and attempt to help again by swinging on the shortest of the three assailants. Connecting to his torso, the punch packs no weight. The attempt makes matters worse for me. The next shot I take to the stomach like the first and has devastating impact. I go crashing into the concrete again. While falling to the pavement, I drift into darkness filled with stars and circles. I begin to lose consciousness. I force my eyes to focus. Dazed, I struggle with all the energy left to stand to my feet.

"Squab fa yo'z cuz."

On one knee now, I am short-jabbed to the jaw by assailant one, folding me up on my back with my knees bent to my chest. While positioned atop of me, he goes through my pockets.

I blurt, "Fuck you!" and receive one final slap to the face.

It hardly seems a fair fight; we are beyond helpless.

Someone in a parked car across the street shouts "Let's go!" in a deep, rough voice. All three predators jog toward the car and make their escape.

Lying there, looking up at the sky, my mind swarms with thoughts. Then I begin going to pieces when I see Blood trickling down the sidewalk. I remember sitting up feeling nauseous. I try to use my arm to hold me up but I am too weak. I hear someone say, "Don't get up, stay down." Although I can't connect a face to the voice, the words resound over and over in my mind.

"Don't get up, stay down."

I lay in the center of a large crowd that materialized in seconds. I hear voices coming from different directions. Whimpering, Tray utters over and over, "Wait till I tell my brothers, just wait." *Who can I tell?* I think for a moment. My heart is pounding and I feel my Blood thumping in the side of my neck. I start wheezing, trying to catch my breath. As Tray and I lay stretched out on the pavement, a young woman offers us a hand with the look of genuine compassion.

Our attackers have to be fifteen or sixteen years old. Gang banging doesn't discriminate on age, gender, or nationality. I don't know why they jumped on us. I assume it has something to do with Tray's red sneakers, shirt, and hat that display X7. I end up with a deep gash in the back of my head, and a few scrapes here and there, while Tray's wounds consist of speed knots and internal pain from the beating.

Back on the Seven block, a li'l breathless from the rapid jog, we tell everything to Tray's brothers.

"What the... who did this to y'all... ahh fuck Blood... What happened... Yo, yo, nah, what the fuck happened?"

I'm surprised at how his brothers respond to our condition. They question us more than attend to our wounds. Their aggression sends chills of relief down my spine, for our injuries spark their anger. What better form of love can one show than concern for your protection? The best thing about hanging with a gang is that revenge is mandatory, right or wrong. With the gang members, where there's no biological connection except a street sign, they protect me with their lives. Mama just sat on the couch watching Auntie beat me.

Despite the pain from the beat-down, the brothers' plans for revenge feel better. I want to tell Mama, but opt not to. *What were you doing around there...? Go to your room... What did you do?* Not the response I want to hear. My older brother is no protection; his life is consumed with girls and football. Getting my ass beaten has more meaning than I know. It opens doors for me to be loved, protected, and down—part of a family.

The aftermath is more important. Broadway and the Seven

block been at each other's necks long before I came to Phoenix. So after they get all the information from us, they order a cadre of troops out to Broadway to seek revenge. At school the next day, Tray informs me the Sevens were successful in their attack.

After helping Tray in his squabble, his brothers' attitudes change toward me, but in my favor. Waiting in line for the ice cream truck, Blizzard, Tray's older brother, approaches.

"Hay wut up li'l Blood, you need some paper?"

Another night the Sevens are about to go out to eat. Before leaving, Q-Tip rolls the window down and shouts, "We 'bout to grub, iz you hungry?"

I feel closer to them, more involved, and respected. I earn the title "Li'l Homee."

They take me under their wing, but I still have a lot to learn, to earn, and to prove.

One afternoon, a bunch of us are hanging on 17th Street eating some jellybeans. Me, Li'l Tray, and another local kid are sitting on the sidewalk joking about the events of the day. As Tray's older brother Soul approaches us, I notice something out of place. He had blue laces in his shoes. *Why is he wearing those? I thought they didn't like blue.* I wanna ask him. I wanna know what it means, but Soul is so aggressive, he might knock me upside the head for asking. I decide not to bother him with my questions. Instead, I ask Tray.

"Why is your brother wearing blue laces?"

"He purified his flag," Tray said.

*What the hell does that mean?*

Soul walks into our cipher and notices me looking down at the blue laces in his All-Stars. I've nervous now and Tray puts me on the spot.

"D, ask him what you asked me."

*Damn, Tray, why you do that? I don't wanna be a buster and ask.*

*I don't wanna seem like a lame.* Just then, Soul stares me in my eyes and demands, "What?"

I don't say anything, I just point to his shoes, which is more than enough for him to understand my confusion.

"Ahh, this ain't 'bout nothing, li'l homee, just caught a ricket slippin', now he sleepin'."

At this point I still haven't made the connection. I'm always a step behind, but Soul schools me. "The only time you catch the homees wearing flue strings is when we smoke a rip. We only do it for a day, and then we burn them. Don't trip, homee; you'll get some too."

In school, Tray says he has something to tell me later. All day I wonder what it is. I'm actually nervous. After school, his brothers are not there to pick him up. We head home. Halfway there, Tray opens up.

"My brothers told me if you wanna be my friend and keep coming around, you gotta blaim the set. You know, get down with the turf Park South." Simultaneously he makes a one and a seven on both hands.

"You gon' have to get jumped in or put in work. My brothers will show you how to catch Crabs." Initiation for the Sevens usually means taking a beating from the entire gang and hunting Crabs.

*Jumped in?* The way I seen the Sevens courting new recruits left me wondering, *Why do they want to hang with people who beat the crap out of them?*

The beatings look real and scary enough, but it isn't like a typical fight on the street. A recruit will fall to the ground, then be made to stand once again, and then will resume the beat-down. Everything seems rehearsed and staged because it appears so perfect. At a predetermined time, one of the Sevens will shout "Seven up!" ending the beating.

Once over, they will all hug, and congratulate the recruits. Everyone chips in on cleaning the Blood off them. T-shirts soaked with Blood are held high while everyone shouts with praise. Now I know why in Tray's brother's room, they have T-shirts hanging on the walls with similar Blood streaks, the Blood they shed for their turf.

*I don't want that. And eating crabs, I don't know if I can do that, I'm allergic. They must really like me though. They want me to hang with them.*

I ate crabs once before, but was rushed to the hospital with an allergic reaction. I was given a shot to minimize the swelling along with some big-ass pills I resentfully swallowed.

A week later, it's time. While Tray and I test our range with a football on the Seven block, the Sevens swarm me.

"Ayy Blood, we gotta take a ride. Hop yo' ass in the bawr."

Fear surges through me. My legs begin to shake, and my heart thumps. I weigh my options but realize there's none. When I see Tray's not coming, I ask, "Ay Tray, you coming?" I pray he is.

Before he can respond, Soul chuckles, "Nah he ain't go'n, just you home bwoy."

Q-Tip follows with some convincing words, "We'll be right back. Don't trip." Soul tosses a Black button-up shirt at me. *Why do I need this shirt, I have a shirt already.*

"Put this on home bwoy, you might need it." I step inside the green and white '64 Pontiac Catalina. Inside is a female driver who I have never met. I ride shotgun while Tray's two older brothers, Soul and Q-Tip, file in the back. Still unaware of their intentions, I let my imagination coast.

•  •  •

The sun is just beginning to set, and the heat is cooking us like a Thanksgiving turkey. Inside the car, G Len blasts through the speakers and smoke fills every area. At the time, I don't realize that every one of their exhales counts as my hit of the weed. I feel woozy.

While riding, Q-Tip and Soul reduce their voices to almost a whisper. I can't understand them because the bass drowns them out. It gets under my skin because it makes me think of two conspirators scheming on someone, possibly me. During the ride, the unknown female driver never says a word except when she curses at a civilian who almost steps in front of the car.

Our destination is 23rd Avenue. I have never been on this block let alone this neighborhood. "Welcome, Crips cards stay hard" is spray-painted on a wall at the beginning of the block. It is unnerving. *Why are we over here?* As we continue down the block, the driver lowers the music just in time for me to catch the end of Soul and Q-Tip's conversation. "He ain't ready. If we get caught, don't nobody know nobody," Soul orders. This spins over and over in my head. *Get caught for what?*

"You ain't spot no C-food yet?" Soul asks the driver a bit frustrated, before taking another drink of beer and another drag from the brown paper bag. *Inhale . . . exhale . . . inhale . . . hold it, hold it, hold it, exhale . . .* I want to know what they're thinking, but everyone's too quiet. I don't know how to break the silence.

"Who we lookin' for?"

Q-Tip, without a doubt feeling the effects of the ganja, shoots back, "Don't mad'da." Then Soul hands the brown paper bag to the driver. Putting the bag to her face she takes two deep hits, zoning off.

"Another one bites da dust," Soul chirps while Q-Tip ruffles the top of my head.

Soul instructs the driver to "get that bitch out of the glove box" in a voice a pimp uses to talk to his ho. Without question, she removes a silver-looking object partially covered by a Black bandanna. It is a gun. Then I feel a big solid hand grip my right shoulder.

Soul leans into me and whispers in my ear in a voice I have never heard before. "Bee dem right dere bick'n'it Blood, take this and squeeze bix times. If you wanna be down you gotta get down."

As I try to turn my head, Soul stops me, redirecting my head back to the front, and demands in a low cold voice, "Focus!"

The hair on the back of my neck stiffens. *Focus!* A simple nod of the head, as I try to appear indifferent.

*What do I do? Is this what Tray meant by huntin'?* I fear if I don't follow their plans, I'll be beaten, or worse, left for dead. I'm afraid, *Don't be a coward,* I scold myself. *How will I learn? I can do this.* This gyrates over and over in my mind. I take a couple sips of beer and it takes hold as I welcome a bewildering shot of calm and composure. New thoughts arrive: *This is my chance to prove myself.*

We are now officially in L-Do Crip 'hood.

Scattered around the block, various kids chase each other, while others throw a ball around. They look like they're having fun. *I wish I could play with them right now.*

"There they go," Q-Tip whispers to Soul. Breaking my stare from the kids, I make contact.

"Look at them busters sleeping. Iz you down or wut nigga, I know you ain't punk'n out? Punk mothafuckin' Brabbz rollin' hella deep . . . If they only knew dat dem Sevens on da creep." Soul rhymes getting amped. When I connect to the object of Soul's affection, I think CRIPS!

The energy in the car is infectious. I nod my head, picking up on it. As we approach four or five boys hanging out on the corner. I hear a strong click sound behind me.

"Here Blood." Soul passes me the gun.

Before I can finish my thoughts, Soul says, "Yeah mothafucka," in a cocky superior voice that sends chills up my spine.

The gun is chrome with Black electrical tape around the handle. I try to zone off and make them see I'm not bitching up, but my nervousness is still in control. As we approach the corner, doing 5 mph, I form my face into the best mask I can find. Seconds before the showdown, with hand and fingers positioned around the gun, my anxiety thickens. I stick my head out the window, aim, and meet the eyes of the fool closest to the curb. I close my eyes, draw in one last breath. *There's no turning back.*

Pop . . . Pop . . . Pop . . . Pop . . . Pop . . . Pop . . . click, click . . . Pulling the trigger gives me a hypnotizing power that surges through my extended arm, up my shoulder, and down my back. My ears ring as my gun pukes its contents. After the initial shot, in the car, egging me on, I hear "Yeah Blood! blast dem mothafuckas!" The first shot is the hardest. Soul and Q-Tip cheer me on from the inside as I continue to fire. Crips start running every which way. Somewhere around my third shot, I feel like I'm playing Duck Hunt on Nintendo. Everything seems to reduce in speed. "Agghhh shit run!" Crips' bodies crumble after each shot. Needless to say, all the practice from Duck Hunt paid off because I am on. I feel a connection that no other feeling can replace, jubilation at its purest and ripest form. It's the utmost penalty man can physically give and receive, and I'm behind it. I now have the power.

"Be out, be out Blood!" Soul shouts as soon as the gun stops, Q-Tip reaches over me, and snatches it away. During the ride back, I try to recollect what just happened. But Q-Tip and Soul keep shouting "Blood was in a fuckin' zone! That's what the fuck I'm talkin' 'bout! Sevens shakin' shit!"

It's hard to digest their praise, for my conscience is condemning me. I feed off their energy with little grins and smirks to show them I'm not fazed. In minutes, we pull up to the Seven block.

I take a moment to ask myself what I have done. I cannot find an answer. Exiting the car, I'm impressed by the welcome I get from everyone. I'm known and recognized now. My name has made a mark here. The Seven block's finest. Sho Nuff, Righteous, Lady Killer, Bam, Li'l Bam, Seven-up, Li'l Seven, B-Boy, She Devil, and Rabbit. Everyone is watching me for any signs of "is he gonna fold on us?" This is my interview, my first impression, my opportunity for acceptance.

They hold a victory celebration for me inside. Drinks, weed, and whatever is in that brown paper bag is available. I feel guilty about what I did, but the exhilaration outweighs my disturbance. Not wanting to appear lame, I take a few more swigs of the beer. I experience pure unadulterated power and it sticks with me from here on out. B-Boy puts $50 in my pocket. Lady Killer continuously praises me, twisting her fingers up in my face in a friendly manner.

"Blood'n ain't easy homee. If you wanna be down you gotta stay down. You gotta earn yo' respect out here, you flow? You flow wit' me?"

I don't get to answer because Soul interrupts. "You gotta fight, shoot, steal, stab, and anything else it takes. We at war with the Rickets." *West Side City.* "They don't give a fuck how young you iz; they'll smoke yo' ass. So instead, we gon' blast dem up first. If you ain't down to squab for yo's Blood, den you buster like Blood." Processing his speech I, with a wide grin, try to appear unmoved so as to not show weakness.

Tray approaches me after Soul's pep talk. "How was it?" *You knew the whole time where I was going.* Before leaving the Seven block that night, Soul hustles over to me and tells me 'hood shit stays in the 'hood. Before I turn and walk away, he throws up the 17th Street sign, and waits for me to respond.

Gracious that he acknowledges me, I return the greeting with a one and a seven. He shows me a few signs, and how to diss down other sets.

"Tomorrow, I'm a show you how to strike up the 'hood." Striking up the 'hood, I heard Tray mention a lot. In fact, I was with him a few times he put the spray cans to use. I'm spellbound by Soul's words, actions, and acceptance.

On the way home, my stomach is queasy. But the Seven block's embrace is rewarding. I feel good. Turning off 17th Street onto Chipman, I practice throwing 17th Street up exactly how Soul showed me. Passing an SUV, I spot a glimpse of myself, and the seven I throw up in the window. Backing up to take a better look at my reflection, I extend my pinky and thumb using my right hand, and hold it to my chest. Fuck daddy! I see myself in a different light. A new image. I'm down.


Stepping in the house, I head straight to my room. The adrenaline finally drains from me, leaving me fatigued. It's difficult to get comfortable because David hogs the bed. But I force my eyes closed with hopes of abandoning the horrific images, but they take a liking to the darkness in the back of my lids. Even though the sharp pain in my heart is hard to swallow, the new coat over my stomach tells me I can do it again.

My heart gradually finds its way back to the traditional beat of boom, boom, boom. I'm left with the indescribable flashes of the destruction I caused. I go through every feasible rationalization my ten-year-old mind can conjure up to justify my actions. Nothing surfaces except, *Why did I do that? Are those people dead?* I remain open-eyed the entire night. My mind shouts back, in an effort to defend myself.

Soul's words resound again in my head, "Focus . . . Focus . . . Focus . . ." The confusion of regret and acceptance gives me a throbbing headache. In time, I realize this night marks my first recorded separation from self. The moment I pulled the trigger, I'm broken and forever changed. After this day, I know violence equals power, and love.

When I wake up the next morning, I am my mother's son again, not the person from yesterday. My stomach is settled but my head is pounding.

At school, Tray appears to be just another kid, but the flag he wears should have been a sign. VII sparked up all over his backpack, notebooks, and sneakers. He always makes reference to the number seven in any and every discussion he has.

"I put it on seven, or word to the sevens."

I always wonder what-all Tray had done for the Seven block. I will never find out. During the end of our fourth-grade year, Tray is caught in crossfire and killed during a drive-by shooting.

We are both eleven years old.

# THE RUDE AWAKENING

*Mommy's grown and her own woman*
*Time she always made to love me*
*Love can blind the receiver at times*
*Blind me from the truth*
*For Mommy abused her soul*
*Easing the pain of rocking me to sleep*
*Loud enough to wake the dead*
*Fall Mommy did*
*For me to wake up and see the dead*

It's time to go. Two weeks after Tray is killed, we pack up again, and move back to the East Coast. After losing my best friend, my identity, and my innocence in Phoenix, I wonder why we've moved to this new place. We don't have any family or friends here; no support. Mom is just doing what she knows best, running. But with all I've been through I don't really know who I am anymore. In Glen Burnie, Maryland, I receive a rude awakening.

Glen Burnie is unquestionably different from Phoenix because the residents are predominately White, with a handful of Black families. I notice that the White kids dress differently. They sport Wrangler jeans, with button-up shirts, sweaters, and penny loafers, or some whack-ass kicks. I wear khakis and plaids thanks to the Phoenix dress code, and I still rock my Jersey style: baggy pants, Timberlands, and long white tees.

Enrolling in the Glen Burnie school system is a major challenge because I am one of only two Black kids in my class and one of eight in the entire school.

Here, I find myself again feeling like an alien in a foreign land.

I become shy and reluctant to speak because I think everyone was more hung up on my skin color than what I had to say. So I hold back, unwilling to share my ideas or ask questions.

Every time I move, speak, or raise my hand, I feel the heat of everyone's eyes. They watch me closely. When I'm called on in class I stiffen my shoulders and recoil. I'm the new kid, and still traumatized by Tray's death. Although the shock never completely subsides, this experience stings like an infected wound next to Tray; it's the second blow in what would become a seemingly endless series of devastations. Readjusting is the bigger factor here; it's getting beyond my skin color.

Glen Burnie confronts me with social challenges that didn't exist in my previous all-Black schools. The less educated you were in both Phoenix and Jersey, the hipper you appeared to be. Learning that my native tongue is "politically incorrect," I discover that my classmates don't speak my language, Ebonics. Vernacular like "ya feel me . . . nahmean . . . str8 like dat . . . word up . . . hol' me down . . . ya dig . . . sike . . . and fasho' fly over my classmates' heads.

Gradually, I learn to speak their language, and it becomes easier for me to adjust. I can't help but think that everything I had learned was either wrong or unacceptable. I am constantly being corrected in front of the class, or I find humor in things that nobody else does. Sometimes I avoid leaving the class when I need to use the bathroom, out of fear that my absence will give them the opportunity to bad-mouth me behind my back. I have good reason to be suspicious. I hear the derogatory things they say about the other Black students. One day, after passing a couple of classmates on the stairway, I overhear them. They laugh at a Black student and his cheap sneakers.

Glen Burnie opens my eyes to many things including racial confusion. It makes me question the value of my skin color and tricks me into feeling inferior. The significance of the word nigger meant nothing to me in Jersey; we said it all the time. Here though, it doesn't hold the same meaning.

Reality hits me when I realize my teacher overlooks me whenever I raise my hand. In class, students can volunteer for extra-credit assignments at the end of the period by whoever raises their hand first for that particular project. Many times my hand bolts in the air first. I am ignored.

In time, I meet a few neighborhood kids who are White. I guess it's safe to say I want to hang with them because I crave many of their prized possessions, gadgets, and games. They seem to have it all: dirt bikes, luxury remote control cars, go-carts, pellet guns, and all the latest video games and systems. Sega Genesis is the hottest game around, and the only time I get to play is when I am in the company of the White kids. I envy their sovereignty and yearn for their better life that shelters them from my contaminated life.

I find myself on the receiving end of their humor. I can see their sarcasm seeping through as they laugh among themselves at their inside jokes.

In November 1992, I experience my cruelest initiation to the world of bigotry.

The fall daylight is coming to an end. A few of the White kids in the neighborhood, kids I think I've gotten to know, plan to go on a mission in an abandoned apartment. They invite me to join them on the adventure. Once we step on the property, someone closes the fence that surrounds the house and quietly locks it. Then the shortest boy of the group nudges a taller boy as they shoot each other conniving grins. *What the hell was that?*

Looking at me, the leader of the group says, "Hey, nigger, you dropped something." I'm curious about his sudden change of tone. His cheeks now seem redder. The word nigger sounds wicked coming from his mouth. Knowing I hadn't dropped a thing, I don't look down. To my surprise, they back me up against a tree and begin kicking soccer balls at me. *Why are they doing this . . . I gotta get outta here.* It appears they are working up enough courage to attack me.

I stand my ground and wait out the assault, smacking the balls aside in succession. *What did I do?* Finally, they seem to lose interest in their attack and stop. The gate is opened and I'm allowed to leave. Fighting back isn't even an option. My pride is shattered. I know how to physically defend myself: But what about the punch you can't see coming? What about the pain that's not physical? The pain that lands directly in a place you can't see, or touch. My heart has never been trained to fight off this type of attack.

Though physically unhurt, my spirit is broken. I'm just a little boy. As an outsider in this foreign environment, all I want is what any kid wants—friends and acceptance. With no Daddy around, and few Black people to identify with, I'm already behind the eight ball. Even so, I thought these guys were my friends. I trusted them. *Why had they done this to me? Was it because I'm Black?* At home, I rack my brain trying to figure out their intentions. Why, I ask my mother through tears, had they betrayed me? *Why did we even have to move here? I hate it here. I'm different. They don't like me.* She hugs me. But it's small comfort, for the experience changes me. I become suspicious of all people, particularly White people.

As painful as this experience is, it teaches me two excellent lessons about the reality of Black and White relations. I learn that being accepted is not something I feel, and two, being Black is equated to having cooties by the White people I've met. I begin believing they are superior, which means I have to become tougher, tougher than anyone.

A few days later, I see the ringleader strolling in my housing complex. My fist is clenched while I shoot him my most evil stare. *I should get cha ass; you think I forgot. I'm a make an example outta you.* My fury burns like fire. I make my way over to him calm and collected. To my surprise, he extends his hand. *Huh! Did he forget? Does he remember me?* I am certain he was there and now is my chance to get even.

"You don't remember me?" Before he can answer, I serve him. Crack!

Blood squirts on my shirt. He grabs his face in pain. I'm aware he's bigger than me so I'm cautious not to give up the control I just secured. He jumps back up and swings. His punch connects to my face but doesn't faze me. *That's all you got?* One-on-one. His high-class world vs. my life of pent-up anger and feelings of abandonment. He stands no chance. I'm Black and I'm furious. I counter with a left jab across his face, and knock him down again. Fear dilates his pupils. Blood is everywhere. He's already accepted defeat, but I've just begun. My attention is riveted on him. As he tries to stand again, I smash the heel of my hand into his nose.

He screams like a girl and then collapses to the street.

Moving in, swinging relentlessly, I bang him in the torso, face, and stomach. I stand up, and yell. "Stand the fuck up, how you like that shit!" I follow with a sharp kick to his face. "Aagghh!" he cries. I don't feel a bit of remorse for him. In fact, I enjoy his pain. I enjoy being superior to him. I want him to feel my pain. He's the big joke now—my joke. Every punch is followed by a slur. "Bitch . . . hate chu . . . fight back . . . I'm a kill you." Still not satisfied, I thrash him some more. He mutters something through the Blood in his mouth, but I don't comprehend his words; they're like gurgles from a baby.

Finally, I snap out of my trance, I climb off him. I watch all the Blood he's soaked in. I spit on him.

"Now mothafucka!" I'm pleased.

"I'm not a nigger," I say. "My name is Dashaun."

The next morning I wake up and my head is clear. My balls have returned to normal size. My body is sore. My hands are bruised from the beating they issued. Job well done. I'm proud.

My younger brother sees me in pain as I move my hands with caution.

"What happened?" I give him the details of the beating.

Glen Burnie alters my life. I find it extremely hard to focus in school. I hate this city, I don't know my mother. I don't know my father. I don't know myself. I become allergic to laughter and humor.

I become intensely introverted and miserable with myself, certain that my life is destined to be a failure. Gradually what I had accepted as truth becomes evident to others: that I am simply one of the unfortunate breed. I believe that the human race produces a select few misfits, general embarrassments, and I am one of them. I feel hopeless.

I have a nightmare about the shooting in Phoenix and Tray. I wake up from a dream rattled with horror. As I lay in bed breathing hard, drenched in cold sweat, the dream fades into my subconscious. Within a minute, I can barely recall what the dream is about. But whatever it was, it leaves me feeling scared. I climb out of bed and shuffle to the bathroom, keeping the lights off so I don't wake

Mama. A murky, humanoid shape moves in the mirror. I let out a cry and quickly flip on the light. There's nothing there. Just me, nervous and gaping at my reflection with puffy, frightened eyes.

"Dashaun?" Mama asks in a scratchy voice. "You okay?"

*No, I'm not okay. I'm seeing shit in mirrors and there's nothing there.*

"I'm okay."

"Thought I heard you shout."

"I'm . . . I'm fine."

My mind is trippin', but I can't explain why.


It's a new morning and my alarm sounds. Light falls on my face. I awaken, muffle a yawn with my pillow, and do a full body stretch. My mood from the night before resumes, I'm already in a funk. With a deep sigh, I press the pillow more securely under my cheek, dreading the day that lies before me, and stare at the ceiling.

I head to the shower. Afterward, I attempt to eat a bowl of cereal, but once again, no milk. *I ain't eating this shit with water no more, fuck that!* Looking in the fridge is like looking in Mom's purse for dough. Empty. I can't understand why there's more Old Milwaukee in the fridge than food. Boy am I hungry this morning, but today will be another day of waiting until lunchtime to eat. After eating watered-down cereal for so long, school lunch is like dining out.

As bad as school is, it's better than being home. I'm more athletic than the rest of my peers and they admire me for that. I am the captain of the football and basketball teams. I believe they start respecting me out of fear. In class, I don't speak; I don't participate, and I zone off a lot.

Lunchtime is torture. I can't afford the paid meals. Every day hardy, mouthwatering food passes me by. As I nibble on the

Sloppy Joe slapped down on my tray, my classmates enjoy various meals. It's embarrassing being on the free lunch plan. There's a small number of free lunch students anyway, and being the three Blacks in line, we all stand out like sore thumbs. A few times, I choose not to stand in line so I won't be humiliated.

Since school started, one thing I hate is going home. Chances are my mom isn't there. One afternoon I come home after school in a decent mood. Derrick's bus from school hasn't arrived yet. That's weird because he normally beats me home. Heading upstairs, I open the door to my mother's room. A foul odor escapes. Pushing the door open, I see her lying in bed with a lighter and a strange-looking bottle wrapped with aluminum foil still in her hand. Her top is partly open, revealing one of her breasts. Her hair is a mess. The image freezes me for a split second. I am shocked and scared. Next to her, a cigarette is burning, and she has foam around the creases of her mouth. Biting my knuckle to stem my own gag reflex, I step inside. I'm careful not to wake her. I inch closer to take a better look. I can't make out what the bottle is. She doesn't even look like herself. *What should I do?* Her skin has turned blue. Her eyes stare blindly at the ceiling.

I stand twisted in silence before running out. I storm into the living room, grab the picture of my mother off the counter, and toss it across the room.

As night closes in, I lie in my bed crying. Once again, I am destroyed, and I have no proper way to deal with this trauma. The next day, I think about asking Mama about what I saw last night, but am too afraid. I don't know what to say or how to ask. For some unknown reason, I think I will be downsized for posing such a question. For the next few days, I'm very distant from her. When in her presence, I sneak a few peeps at her to see if she is acting weird.

Coming home from school, a few days later, upstairs, I can hear Mama has company in her room. From the deep harsh voice I gather it's a man. Approaching the door, I lean in closer. They are speaking too low, almost whispering. I figure he has to come out. *What are they doing in there? Why are they whispering?* An hour or so later, the door opens and I meet the eyes of this stranger. Something about his presence makes me cringe inside. He stands well over six feet, but what's distinctive about him is his missing tooth and foul breath. As he approaches me downstairs where I purposely sit, he says coldly, "Hey dere li'l man, wassup?" *Not you.* Then he reaches his hand out to lock with mine. I am hesitant to meet him halfway but he is an adult.

"Nothing."

As he shakes my hand, he takes a big sniff wiping his nose with the other hand before patting me on the head. I burn with fury, wishing I had enough strength to flatten him. I take a deep breath which expands my chest. I want him to think I am not fazed by his rude gesture. As I watch him walk out the front door, he looks back at me and says, "Lock the do'."

Later on that night, Derrick and I are subjected to an interrogation.

"Who went in my room? Where's my money?"

I didn't go in her room and Derrick denies it. *Maybe it was that stinky guy you let in the house.* But at this moment, saying something like that is suicide. Judging by the veins in her neck, silence is best. Convinced that we'd stolen the money, she continues to scream at us.

"I'm not gonna ask again. Who went in my room?"

She bangs drawers in her room, ransacking everything. Now she's checking the bathroom. No luck, she slams the door shut.

Plates in the kitchen find their way to the floor. Next stop my room. She rummages through my drawers and closet. *A smack is coming.* I make sure I keep a good distance between us.

"This place is a fucking mess. That's why I can't find anything.

Why don't y'all clean this mess up?" The more she searches the harder she fumes. Derrick and I listen to her tear through the house. Then she comes back to our room. Her hands are planted on her hips and her mouth is scrunched so tightly you can barely see her lips. Her eyes are large and vacant. *No one would think she was nice if they saw her now.*

"Clean this room up!"

After giving up her search, she slams our door and leaves the house. She's gone. I lie on my stomach in my bed and cry.

In the sixth grade, my teacher sends a note home complaining about my lack of participation with the other kids. "Dashaun is antisocial. He's impolite to the other students and not willing to participate." When my mother questions me, I think to myself, *Every friend that I ever make, you move me from. Why should I make friends with people who don't like me? The few friends I do have, I won't have for long because we'll move again.*

I create my own entertainment. I begin writing in a journal. Within a week, my notebook is full. Everything from drugs and alcohol, to racism, my father, and to Tray. I write about my mother's addiction while trying to keep my classmates from hearing my stomach growl.

*Today is Friday, and my class is going on a field trip to some stupid park. I gotta sit in the classroom till they come back. It cost twenty dollars to go but my mom don't got no money. I don't care because I don't wanna go anyway.*

Being one of the poor kids only adds to my misery.

Most afternoons, I hang out with Bump, Jizzo, Maurice, and OJ, avoiding my house. We are five of the eight Blacks in my school.

We spend our time in the woods with Bump's two pellet guns, one of which is a rifle, shooting at cans, birds, and squirrels.

Hunting animals in the woods is a bond that all the Black kids in the neighborhood have. In the woods we search for anything of use. Tic, Bump's older brother, is in high school and has a reputation of being a drug dealer. Snow covers the woods and we toss snowballs at one another. Tic spots a stray dog that clearly hasn't eaten in days. His ribs are bulging through his coat, and his eyes are lazy. Unafraid of the mysterious dog, we decide to throw snowballs at it. Suddenly, Tic pulls out a small .22-caliber handgun and shoots the dog behind the ear. We all jump back in fear. As the dog falls to the ground, there's a cloud of steam when the warm blood hits the cold air. The dog jerks from side to side and a big wet bubble comes out of its nose. Then it lies still. I stand and watch, along with everyone else, as the dog dies.

One afternoon, riding my bike in my neighborhood I see in the distance a giant figure coming directly toward me with no intentions of moving. His frame increases in size as he gets nearer. Before I know it, he stands hovering over me.

"Get the fuck off!" he demands with a push that lands me on the concrete. Looking up, I see the culprit mounting my bike. With fear running through me, I retrieve my pellet gun on my waist, and aim it at the perp trying to escape. I size his body up in my shooting range.

Pop! Pop! Pop!

He falls off my bike while clutching his ass. Tears stream down his face as he repeatedly screams, "Aagghh! Owww! Owww! You shot me!" With him reeling in pain on the ground, I Jackie Chan him with a karate kick to the side of his neck. The kick feels better than actually shooting him. I climb on my bike and pedal home.

My mother isn't home when I get there, which is a good thing. I immediately stash the pellet gun in the backyard, safe from authorities, and tell my brother what happened. I look out the window, nervous that the bike thief'd come for retaliation.

An hour later, after my nerves settle, there are two knocks at my door.

It's two White police officers, who both seem intimidating. *Maybe if I don't answer the door they'll leave.* But then the fear of cops makes me feel obligated to let them in. Derrick frantically says, "Are you going to jail? Don't open the door."

Once I open the door, the shorter officer of the two asks for my name. "D-D-Dashaun." My voice is just above a whisper. My palms are sweaty, and my heart kicks into fifth gear, about to burst.

"You have to come with us, you're under arrest." My first time.

Derrick looks on helplessly as the officers cuff and usher me off into the squad car. *I don't wanna go to jail.* When I get to the car, I'm fearfully banging on the window. As we make our way out of the complex, a few neighborhood kids wave to me as I'm driven away.

East Glen Burnie Juvenile Detention Center houses all juvenile delinquents.

I'm twelve years old, so my mom is able to pick me up. The injured vic's parents choose not to press charges, lucky for me, but I'm ordered to perform one hundred hours of community service. When the detective informs me that my mama is on her way to pick me up I think, *Ooooh nooo!* I sit in panic the whole time. I remain on a bench next to the holding cell. When she finally arrives at the Juvenile tank to pick me up, she's outraged. The door to the holding area finally opens, and Mama jacks me up by the collar. I'm sure she's going to kick my ass here, but she leaves me with just the anticipation of the beating until we reach home. There's a huge pulsating vein protruding through the center of her forehead. She's noticeably more intimidating than usual. Her anger speaks volumes through her flesh.

During the ride home, Mama makes vague references about me learning my lesson. "What's wrong with you boy . . . see what you done . . . what do you have to say for yourself?" Little did she know, I had been changing for a long time, right under her nose.

As a result of my run-in with the law, Mama grounds me. I hate being confined and, years later, it would drive me mad.

I don't understand what I did wrong. I'm infuriated because she won't allow me to explain why I defended myself. The guy never once mentioned to the cops that his plan was to stick me up. When I tell Mama, I'm reduced to silence with a slap across the face. I choke back my anger and remain quiet.

What trips me out is hearing what he told the cops. After I shot him, I allegedly kicked him, which I did, went in his pockets, a lie, and confiscated $50 and a pager, another lie. It's crazy how one's emotions can change so quickly. My attitude went from hate to love and empathy for my mother in a matter of days. Soon, my mother's life and mine would change forever.

One day after school, around 3:30, my brother and I walk into the house. Heading toward the stairs, I glimpse the bathroom light on. Without hesitation, I turn off the costly electricity and, to my surprise, I find Mom passed out in the bathtub. I begin to panic. I cry.

"Mom wake up! Wake up! What's wrong! Say something to me!" I'm petrified that my mom is going to die. I can hear my li'l brother crying behind me, but it sounds like echoes from a distance.

He pulls the back of my shirt, "Let me see . . . what's wrong . . . move . . . Mommy!"

*Why won't you wake up?* The whole episode feels surreal, like a nightmare that's supposed to happen to someone else. Looking around the bathroom awkwardly, not knowing what to do, I struggle to control my own anger, I feel incapable of helping my mother.

My aunt Claudette, who is visiting, comes running down the stairs two and three at a time to see what all the commotion is about. At the first sight of my mother, she too begins to panic. I can't help but notice that my mom's face is Black-and-blue again. I sit there stunned and confused, until the sound of Auntie yelling "Wake up Angie . . . come on now . . . we gotta get up . . ." jars my attention. My mother's eyes have rolled back in her head, her tongue hangs out. Auntie stays by my mother's side all night nursing her back to herself.

I cry silent tears the entire night in my room, alongside my brother. Once you've seen your everything look busted down to nothing, it devalues you, and deadens your soul. From this event forward, I carry this image of my mother's Black-and-blue face, her hanging tongue. I took all of my resentment, anger, and frustration that was occurring, bottled them up, and forced them deep down inside of me.

I realize that the one person who's supposed to help me sort out my feelings is not there. She's locked in a dark room.

Mama didn't speak of my father, almost like she was keeping him a secret. I know everyone has a dad and I want to know where mine is. I imagine what he's like, what he looks like, and why he never comes to see me. I lie in my bed sketching pictures of him and me. My brothers, Derrick and David, have different fathers that they met. I don't even have my dad to turn to. Since I have no idea of his identity, sometimes he's dark-skinned, long-haired, heavy, and wealthy, while at other times he's light-skinned, bald, lean, and poor.

During my fifth-grade year, my missing father becomes a problem.

It is dress-up day in school. While my mother did her best to fill the void left by my absent father, she's unable to properly knot my tie. My fellow students make fun of my sloppiness. That evening I lie in bed convincing myself that had my father been there, I would have been spared the embarrassment.

In March, Mrs. Tully, my fifth-grade teacher, gives the class a homework assignment for Father and Son Day. I'm thrilled, believing that Mama will now have no choice but to call my dad. *Why wouldn't she?* My teacher says our fathers have to come as an assignment for class. Eager to see my mother, I hurry home and excitedly tell her the news. I have every intention of finally getting to meet this mysterious man.

"Mom guess what? It's Father and Son Day at school. Can you call Daddy so I can bring him to my class?"

As she blows puff after puff of her Newport cigarette smoke around me instigating cough after cough from me, she says ruefully, "He ain't gonna come." It takes a moment for the import of her words to sink in.

I'm not satisfied with her answer, but there's no other answer to be found.

"Why?" I say nonchalantly,

"Look, he won't be coming but I can go if you want me to." The excitement I built up is sucked out of me.

"Mommm, it's Father and Son Day and you're not my dad."

Wishing I could have taken a sick day from school, I reluctantly make my way into the classroom. For a second, I wonder why my older brother couldn't fill in for my father. He's seven years older than me and I know he can pass for my father, but then I realize I haven't seen David in weeks.

The day of the assignment, while each father accompanies his son to class, I sit alone with *Bastard* written all over my face. I vividly remember watching all my classmates go in front of the class and recite what their father's professions are. My classmates explain how their fathers are their role models, they talk about the hiking trips they go on, the fishing trips they take. When my name is called to present, everyone looks at me with the expression of "Where's your father?" In a slightly low-key voice, I say, "He couldn't come."

My teacher then says in a cold voice, "That's fine, just come to the front and present him anyway."

*You tell me what the hell am I going to present dumb-ass. I don't even know what the fool looks like.* I decline and say once again, "He's not here." By now I feel degraded.

"I can't hear you!" she says trying to lure me to the front of the class. My embarrassment feels like a ton of bricks on my back and I feel paralyzed from the waist down. I want to cry but my face won't cooperate. I feel like she enjoys embarrassing me.

I repeat myself again, louder this time: "He couldn't fuckin' come!" followed by an irritated sigh and a choice word: "Shit!"

I receive an F. I don't get the F for not having my father present; I get that grade because of my foul language and for storming out of the classroom.

I don't understand how I'm supposed to be a "regular boy" when I don't have a father. *There's something wrong with me. God doesn't like me.* I try to make some distant memory of my father resurface. I want to know what he smells like, if he bites his nails, or if he's ticklish. I want to know everything about him. Mama won't tell me.

Mama works two jobs, sometimes three, to make ends meet. Cleaning White folks' homes, bussin' tables, and changing pissy bedpans at nursing homes. Mama is hardly home because of the hours she works. When she is there, it's like she's not. She's distracted by her own world.

It's a lost cause to not know where you stand in life. I'm thirteen, and already I feel I have no identity, no history, and no future. I am in turmoil, not knowing whether I'm coming or going. Once again, change has its way with me as my mother does what she's best at: move.

# THE 90'Z

*Playground of the devil are where dead leaves play*
*Blown away from a tree never to call my own*
*Colors of bright another life ago*
*A lonely draft without aim*
*Drifting further from the sun*
*Joy of mind is to be numb*
*Tone has altered for winter has come*
*Night falls when leaves sing*
*A song of death*
*Piles of overflowed emotions*
*For no one wants leaves upon their blanket*
*No match for none, for winter is angry*
*Survival will be the leaf*
*Together we pile for warmth*
*The one leaf no longer blows*
*Dear winter has consumed*
*My friend no longer changes color*

THE WAR IS ON — BOTH THE HIGH-STAKES BATTLE IN THE STREETS
and the silent one raging within me. Caught up in storms of con-
flict, I find my swagger and fight. For respect, for revenge, for my

life, and too often for all the wrong reasons. Inside, I feel like a loser, but on the battlefield I am an asset. At home I am nobody, but in the 'hood, I am the man.

After a year and a half in Glen Burnie, my mother decides it's time to move. Our destination is our origin: Irvington, New Jersey. While I was away, guns and knives have made their way into the 'hood. There are no Bloods and Crips; just posses and cliques.

Moving back home is not an easy transition. I return a completely different person than when I left. I had embarked on a path lined with violence, loneliness, and dark moods. I loathe being without a father. I feel isolated and unwanted. I develop new insecurities that never existed before.

When I arrive home, I'm greeted by many of my old neighborhood comrades including JP, Smitty, Rel, Mikal, Dawoo, Li'l D, Killa, and Dallas. As soon as they see me they notice my unusual style of dress. Khakis and Chucks. Once again, I feel like a foreigner, only this time in my hometown.

The year is already off to a bad start.


My mother, brothers, and I move back in with my aunt Claudette on Breckenridge Terrace. Auntie has always been there for us. She and Mama are best friends. When we needed a place to live, she took us in.

I enroll back into Grove Street School where there are quite a few new faces. In the neighborhood, hopping roofs, stealing bikes, and shooting hoops in Grove Street playground is a typical day's fun.


We start out as a loosely knit group of edgy young'stas who share a passion for many of the same things. The ties we form while causing trouble evolve into friendships. The backbone of the group is comprised of JP, the toughest; Li'l D, the rowdiest; Rel, the quietest; and me, the inspirational leader. I'm the one who has no trouble conceiving a plan and executing it. Our territory covers three blocks bound by Grove Street, Breckenridge, Tichenor, and 18th Avenue. Grove Street housed the most dominant block, the HQ. Our neighborhood park resides on this stretch of road that hosts our physical aggressiveness. Our most common activity is jumping roofs. We are fearless daredevils who will jump between thirty-foot-high roofs separated by six-foot alleys. We soup each other up to jump from one building to another. Sometimes we are up so high, a fall would guarantee death. But we don't care; we soar over every roof in the neighborhood, from stores to abandoned buildings, and we get chased by the cops for wreckless mayhem throughout the city.

Posses and cliques have developed into organized crews, and who you kick it with largely defines you. While I was away, the customary street squabbles and the traditional style of going at it from the shoulders became outdated. The new way of handling your business substitutes good old-fashioned fistfights with knives and guns. If you can't stand up for yourself in my 'hood, if you can't bang, you are considered dry, weak, a punk. You are looked down upon, laughed at, beat up, and humiliated. Knives give you rank in the hierarchy, but you still have to establish yourself physically by proving your knuckle game and confronting all disses.

Big is a huge cat I used to hang with. He resembles the rapper Biggie Smalls. He's from 18th Avenue and when I came back, he had organized a clique called Black Mafia. These hooligans roll through elementary school together, twenty and thirty deep every day. After school is when they randomly harass and tap everybody's pockets. In addition to their day-to-day routine, they are at war with their biggest enemy, the Haitians.

Irvington treats 'hood combat with the utmost seriousness,

amassing arsenals and planning tactical strikes like the military.

The word has spread throughout the 'hood that the Haitians are going to kill a 40 Boy.

Drag, an older guy on my block, is one of the founders of the 40 Boyz. The clan started with forty kids from 40th Street and Springfield Avenue. The 40s are older and all go to Irvington High and Myrtle Ave Middle.

I'm quick to learn that my posse GST, Grove Street, is among many crews who fight against the Haitians. So I get to know who is who, and what is what. After school we get into scuffles with fools from other blocks. We are all down for each other, and defend our turf.

Elementary school is a significant period for me because I learn the physical power I possess.

JP is the toughest member of the group.

I was born a year and a half after JP, but soon grow to his height. JP is like a big brother to me but he always tests me with physical confrontations, and I hate it. He's done this since the first grade. Now that I'm back in town, things change.

One day JP continuously agitates me by pushing and hounding me. His luck is about to run out.

"Chill out," I repeat countless times, but he keeps pushing. Prior to that day, I had never challenged nor attempted to get the best of him because I knew what the outcome would be. JP is impetuous, outgoing, fond of his popularity, and demonstrative with his feelings. I'm the opposite: reserved and quiet. But things changed over the course of three and a half years. I have a lot more anger inside me now than I outwardly demonstrate. I have seen and been through things in the past few years that not only outweigh his strength, but add to mine.

An enormous surge of rage builds up in me this particular day. His last push sends an explosion through me, releasing a Hail Mary right to the kisser. He's stunned. I catch a glimpse of his confusion while he goes down. I feel like a mountain has been lifted off my shoulders.

"Yeah!" I shout in victory.

Post KO, reality sets in and my guts suggest I disappear. I hurry across the street to Shoes's house. Shoes is an older guy that lives on the block. He's like an uncle to the neighborhood kids. After a minute down, JP gets to his feet, and comes to Shoes's house looking for round two, but Shoes isn't gonna let me come out. JP and I are practically family, and family beefs are something Shoes is adamant about squashing. I don't think I would have gone out, regardless. I know that with all the anger JP has now, he'll beat my ass. Anyhow, the excitement of manning up to him and putting him down changes me, empowers me. As I watch him and Shoes talk on the front porch from the living room window, I pace back and forth in somewhat of a victorious swagger.

"I bet he won't fuck wit' me no mo'!"

"I ain't takin' no mo' shit from him or nobody else!"

And after that day, he will gain more respect for me as I do myself.

Realizing that my peers have more fun being heartless than noble, I develop bulletproof skin and make note that there are two kinds of people: predators and prey. I choose the former. I have the power to demean and hurt someone. I resort to the use of my hands to gain respect. The reality is that I hate myself, but I take my frustrations out on other people.

Even my mother once warned me, "Don't you know that when another boy hits you, you hit 'em back, and if he's bigger than you, pick something up and knock his ass out with it."

It is important to show others and myself that I am not one to pin my tail between my legs. I will not turn the other cheek.

Coming back to Jersey in the midst of the combat between the 40s and the Haitians is crazy. Now, the Haitians stick together. They wear funny-looking clothes: tropical-colored shirts and off-color pants, strappy open-toed sandals. Most of them smell of curry.

There was no American-Haitian controversy when I left Jersey for Phoenix. Evelow is a Haitian who lives on my block. Years ago, he was considered one of us. When I came back, I found Evelow is cliqued up with the Haitians and fully down for the A-H beef, Americans vs. Haitians. I never get the real story of how the war started, but I know I'm in the middle of it.

Before sixth grade ends, I experience street war for the second time. Phoenix taught me what retaliation meant and Jersey allowed me to excel at it.

Tiger's younger brother Li'l Lep has class with Li'l D and me. Tiger is the leader of the Haities and has an arsenal of riders behind him. Word comes down from Drag, one of the founders of the 40 Boyz, that the night before Tiger underwent a beat-down. Drag issues a green light on all Haitians in school. The elder 40s handle things in Irvington High and Myrtle Avenue, while we, the young'stas, will assault the elementary school. I repeatedly ask Drag for the strap.

"Let me hold it, come on, come on Drag!"

Drag grins. "For what?" He responds in a sarcastic tone.

"To take to school tomorrow, I'm a shoot Lep. I ain't scared of no Haitians."

"Nigga what! Yo, you on some shit, you think you gon' get away wit' shootin' him in class?"

I never even acknowledge his rational thinking.

Not sure if I will shoot Lep. I'm hungry for another taste of that same intense euphoria I felt back in Phoenix when I was respected by the Sevens for the work I put in.

Lep and I are classmates during third period when Li'l D, Smitty, Killa, Mikal, Dallas, Monster, and I muster up a plan to launch our first ambush. We enter the class five minutes late so we know Lep will be a sitting duck. All wearing white tees and Black flags over our faces, we rush the class.

To our surprise, Lep puts up an effort to fight us off. He makes the first move by launching a chair at us, before getting swarmed. More than once I connect my Timberland to his head while the others rearrange his already jacked-up face. While this is going on, my classmates begin scampering from the class in groups of two and three. Lep moans, in obvious pain, and then he suddenly goes into a seizure. This doesn't stop us.

Smitty ends the attack with one last crack to Lep's head with a metal stool. We leave him fucked up, and more important, with a message from the Americans.

Drag is proud of me. "Dae, that's what I'm talking about. Y'all some wild li'l niggas. That's how you handle business. That's how you earn respect. Respect comes from power and power means showing no weakness." Drag gives me a hug as we part. I feel good.

The week following the classroom jump-off, while involved in a group discussion in class, I find fifteen to twenty Haitians rushing the classroom, charging in my direction.

*Oh shit!* I'm assed out. I can't do nothing but accept this ass whooping with open arms. Ironically, the description Li'l Lep gave of me is slightly off because the classmate sitting next to me catches the fade. Rashawn and I do look like each other. As I jump out of my seat ready to defend myself, I hear a Haitian shout, "That's dat mothafucka right dere," while pointing at Rashawn. They beat him down with chains, bats, and brass knuckles. They tear into him like lions on a gazelle. Helping him isn't even an option.

The bad blood between the Haitians and the 40s continues with each camp retaliating for the last strike.

Eight of us are hooping in a Grove Street playground one night around ten when two Haitians unknowingly walk past the playground. Dawoo peeps them first. "Yo, ain't that two Haities right dere?" He's right. Dawoo assumes authority within the clique. He's more experienced. He's thirteen.

Apparently the Haitians think it's safe to catch the late bus leaving Grove, heading toward South Orange Avenue. They never make it. We run after them, catch them at the bottom of Tichenor Terrace, stomp on them like grapes, and then throw them, battered and Bloody, over the parkway.

A week later, the Haitians assemble a stronger counterattack. Riding my bike to Cooper's Sandwich Shop five minutes from my house, I have an urge for a pastrami sandwich. As I return, crossing Grove Terrace, I hear firecrackers.

Pop! Pop!

*What's that? Sounds like a car backfiring.* I jerk from the sound. When I turn onto the block and see Tyson on the ground I think gunshots, they are shooting at us. In spite of the war with the Haitians, and my actions, I wish this would all end. *No; can't be a buster. Be hard. Revenge.*

Tyson will survive the shooting, but will undergo serious therapy to regain full movement and flexibility in his leg.

Dawoo and I swear on the 'hood we'll get revenge first chance we get. We turn the volume up a notch and get clever. We make plans to attack this weekend, two days away. For the rest of the week I think about our mission, rehearsing it over and over in my head, envisioning my role. Dawoo and I already decide what we'll do. Time for history to repeat itself.

Since the war started with the Haitians, I learned that behavior can be camouflaged. I move around the house like nothing's happened. I know I must remain calm and show self-control or my mother may intervene.

"Dashaun, how's school?"

*Well we just fucked up a Haitian and Tyson got shot. I'm angry, and I hate myself, but other than that, I'm fine.*

"It's fine."

"I'm leaving shortly, y'all make sure the dishes are done and the garbage goes out."

"I will."

Seconds later, she's out the door. Inside this house, I feel unwanted, and insignificant. Outside, I feel powerful, needed, and respected.


We ask a female who is in good with the Haities to do some investigative work. Her job is to find the residence of any Haitian, preferably the leader, Tiger. She isn't able to score Tiger's spot; however, we do get the address of another Haitian. The preliminary work pays off.

Our plan is to make two moves. One, commandeer a stolen car, and two, trash the Haitians.

The night of the attack, I wait by the side of my house in the dark for Dawoo to do what he excels at, steal a car. I'm preparing for what's to come. I remember to wear all Black like the Sevens taught me. *Might need it. I could get killed.*

Dawoo pulls up in front of my house. The first part of our plan runs smooth. I creep from the alley behind the stolen Civic and point my fingers at Dawoo, "Stick up!"

Surprisingly, he doesn't flinch. "Aggh, nigga, stop playing. You ready? Let's roll."

I stuff the .38 in my waistband, courtesy of Drag—it's fully loaded and ready to vomit. The barrel is cold against my stomach as I lean back in my seat. Our predetermined location is just across the parkway, behind Myrtle Avenue. We head out. I've been here before I tell myself. I recline in the passenger seat buzzed from a beer.

My heart starts pounding at the thought of what we're about to do. My hands tremble. The world spins. We're heading for trouble. I take another sip of the Olde English. We're going to shoot somebody. I think about my orders from Drag. My heart hammers like crazy. I am another person now. *There's no turning back. I'm in this.*

We ride around our enemy's 'hood. It's dark. I see movement but I can't see faces. But they are there, just as our informant Lisa said. We eye up a crowd of Haities hanging out on the porch of a house.

"There they go," Dawoo whispers. A few feet away from me, two Haitians stand in front of the house, away from the crowd on the porch. "Get them, get them right there," Dawoo says. The Haitians appear to be in their late teens. One is dark-skinned, medium built with a bald head, while his partner is noticeably taller with a low haircut.

We pull around the side. I check my weapon to make sure it's fully loaded and ready.

"You ready?" Dawoo asks.

"Yeah!"

Dawoo drives slowly down the poorly lit block positioning me closest to the house. "Kill the lights," I order Dawoo. This is something the Sevens did in Phoenix whenever they went hunting. When thinking about it, I wonder, *Why dim the lights? Won't that make us look suspicious?* I assumed it was something that gangsters did. It wasn't until years later that I found out that we dimmed the lights to cover the license plates.

I lock in on the two victims like a soldier in training, remembering everything I have to do.

*Focus. Don't punk out.*

We're five feet away.

*There's no turning back.*

As we are within shooting range, I roll down my window, take a deep breath, hold the gun with both hands, and shout "Fuck Haiti!" at the top of my lungs and fire. It's easy. Like shooting cans. Tattattattattattat.

I squeeze repeatedly until there are no more shots. Bits of wood from the house and clods of dirt fly everywhere; glass shatters, sending Haitians diving for cover. Burned powder fills the air. My ears echo with the shots and screams. The two Haitians on the sidewalk twitch and groan.

"That's for Tyson mothafucka!" Dawoo shouts.

My heart pounds faster, my arms and legs are cold. But I'm exhilarated. *I'm the fuckin' man. Who the fuck want it?* The intensity of the battle amps me up.

Dawoo slams on the gas, burning rubber. We keep the lights off until we are clear of all danger and any eyewitnesses. I don't care who I hit as long as they felt our attack. This strike adds to my gaining prestige as a rider.

I spend a few minutes at Drag's reliving the shooting. I turn over the gun, then I dismiss myself from the gang and go home. I fall asleep the moment my head hits the pillow.

When I awake the next morning, I'm Dashaun again, as if last night never happened. I'm my mother's little baby. I brush my teeth and eat a bowl of cornflakes.

I drag the garbage out to the curb. I hear the sounds of a basketball dribbling a few doors down. "You ready," Rel reminds me—it's time to head to school. Suddenly, my stomach turns. I squint my eyes to obliterate the splashing images of the night before, but they play behind my lids. I can't escape. I'm going to vomit.

I see them lying on the ground in pain. Blood covers their shirts. I never thought I'd do it again. This isn't the person I wanna be. It's not how I imagine myself. I can't take back what I've done.

*Who am I?*

Soul's words from my first get-down resound in my head: "If you wanna be down you gotta stay down." The memory of Phoenix fills me with feelings of safety and love.

I can't tell anyone of my feelings of guilt. Riders don't fold. I'm a comrade. I'm thirteen.

I spend most of my time fighting myself mentally in order to avoid thinking about what I have seen and done. The more I resist thinking, the more my head hurts. I become afraid to sleep for fear that my suppressed thoughts will emerge in my dreams.

The war would reach its peak one afternoon as Li'l D, Smitty, Rel, Dallas, Mikal, Monster, and I walk home from school.

A car full of Haitians pulls up. As they get out, we scatter in different directions trying to escape the attack of the older and clearly determined side. Everyone gets away except for Li'l D. They all seem to follow him as he takes them on a foot chase that ends on 16th Avenue and Grove. There's a building where we used to meet up on 16th that I assume Li'l D thinks he can elude them by hiding in. This is a bad decision because about eight or nine of them follow him. He is repeatedly beaten, kicked, punched, and finally set on fire. Mikal, Rel, and Killa meet up with me on Breckenridge still waiting on Li'l D to arrive. As five minutes turn to ten and ten turn to twenty, we realize something is wrong. The police cars, sirens, and fire trucks tip us off that maybe he's in trouble. We follow the cars down Grove where people are lined up everywhere watching on as the paramedics rolled Li'l D out of the building with burns all over his body. He looks really bad and isn't even conscious.

I head to the hospital with Mutah and Deion a few days later to check on Li'l D. When I finally get to see my friend, he's in a tent and his body is covered with a rubber sheet that is spread with ice. He has third-degree burns over three-quarters of his body. I assemble enough courage to look from his hair to his eyes. What I see in his eyes I have never noticed there before. It was fear. Out of the entire clique, Li'l D was the cowboy. His scars told his stories, always in a stolen car, in and out of the hospital for a broken arm here and a dislocated shoulder there. He didn't fear shit and would go a few rounds with Iron Mike Tyson if he could.

More than anything, I want to reach out and hug him, and say, "Please don't die." I want to tell him to be strong, but I don't have the courage because I don't want him to think he is dying. Ironically, I get angry. He is too strong, too tough to be defeated. I tell him that he needs to get up. Decide whether he is going to live or die, because I can't take this straddling-the-fence living-and-dying state that he's in. I even raise my voice out of frustration, and tell him that he is stronger than this! I have, for the first time I can recognize, encountered absolute unconditional love. I stare at his still body and all I want is for him to know that I love him—no matter what! I want to command him to get the fuck up, or die! This was one of the most emotional days of my life.

For two weeks he hovers between life and death. Speaking is a terrible strain for him and the only words I hear him utter are

"Wut up?" and "How I look?" I suppose this was his way of trying to comfort me. Every day I sit with him, I think the same thing: that more than anything I want him to live so we can watch a Haitian burn. I repeat over and over to myself "Fuck dem Haitians," but I can't force the words out. Finally, one afternoon, as I stand up to leave, with a tremendous strain, he says, "Fuck dem Haitians."

A year into living back in Jersey, my mom decides to clean up and enroll in a rehabilitation clinic. My brothers and I find out that she'll be leaving for a month or so. To a child, a month seems forever.

The day she leaves, she tries to make us feel better about her going. She sits Derrick and me down at the kitchen table. "I want y'all to listen to me. Mommy needs some help. I'm going to need for y'all to be strong, and when I get back, things will be different I promise." A van in front of our house takes her away. I watch until the very last minute when she turns off our block.

For eternity, *in real time just over a month,* it's pure torment because she is not able to communicate with us at all. Every night I wonder what she's doing, and if she's thinking about me. I look in the mailbox every day hoping there will be a letter, but nothing. As the days pass by, I isolate myself from the outside world as much as possible. All I want is for my mother to come back. As her arrival date gets nearer, I become more anxious and excited.

Thirty-five days later, she's cleared to be released and start a new life.

The sun is shinning brighter today and seems to embrace her with welcoming warmth as she steps off the van. I run down the steps into my mother's arms. My eyes well with tears as we hug.

My brother tries to squeeze his way in between our hug, but the tightness of the hold forces him to wait his turn. My mother cries. In spite of everything, something is different about Mama. Her eyes glitter like polished rubies, and her smile beams like a million stars. I am proud of her and embrace her again with a hug as if it is my last. I hang all over her, kissing her, telling her how much I love and miss her.

Once back inside, she enlightens us on everything that happened during her absence. The food she ate, where she slept, who she met, and what she learned. As she speaks with words I never heard her use before, I find myself teary-eyed again, but happy. She seems to be a totally different person in the way she looks, dresses, and speaks. She cut her hair and even stopped smoking cigarettes. She prays before eating and going to bed. She reads the Bible, and soon starts going to Tabernacle Baptist Church.

Eventually, my mom's new beliefs are directed at my brother and me. With her changes come new rules.

My brother and I have to be in the house by sundown. She stops approving of the people I hang with and makes us attend church with her. I argue and fight with my mama every day. I don't like the fact that she forces us to go to church every single Sunday. What makes matters worse is we have to walk up Breckenridge, onto 18th Avenue, and pass Ellis Avenue, in order to get to the church on South 20th Street. All my friends live on these blocks, and they can all watch while my mother, brother, and I walk by in our church clothes. This is embarrassing because no one in the 'hood goes to church. Plus, her new rule limits my contribution to the American-Haitian war.

I am not greatly attracted to the church worship services. The hymns are boring and depressing to me. I consider the minister a good man, but his sermons don't hold my attention.

The only memorable religious event for me during her recovery occurs one Sunday morning when the pastor delivers an emotional sermon. Out of nowhere, the man sitting in front of me begins shaking uncontrollably. His body is conquered by more shakes and moves than a man going through convulsions.

I am spooked. I've never witnessed anything of the type before. As I look around, everyone is fanning, crying, and praying along with him. More than anything, it's what it did to my mother that fascinates me. She begins crying and shouting "Hallelujah!" over and over.

I find it difficult to believe in a God who loves each human being personally. That God seems a stranger to me when I consider the size of the world. How can he be interested enough to listen to a ghetto bastard such as myself if I pray?

I never understand how she manages to pray as if she is certain that God actually listens. I want to shake her sometimes, scream at her that she is wasting her time. But I keep my mouth shut and allow her to nurture her illusions. Everyone has to believe in something.

I am protected and shielded by my anger and depression. I feel most comfortable when I'm raging. I get so hot, at times I feel dizzy. Mama tries a few solutions to help me, but nothing seems to work. She tries talking to me and eventually pleads with me to seek professional help, but I oppose the idea fiercely. So instead, her next plan is to do what she always does: move. To her, moving is a solution to her problems.

By the time I am in the eighth grade, I have attended six schools in three different states. For as long as I can remember, I have felt like I don't belong. I still wonder about my father. He runs across my mind a lot even though I never met him. With new emotions added to the old ones, I am on a road that leads to nowhere. So I add a new chip on my shoulder, and say "FUCK THE WORLD!" As I move on to a new place, my life takes a new path.

# CITRUS HILL

*Prepared I am for my new world to be*
*For difference are the faces*
*They begin a game I know best*
*An ugly past is now to be my war paint*
*In a town named a fruit I have chosen to die*
*Sweet is to be everything but tight in my eyes*

DURING HIGH SCHOOL, MY LIFE TRULY BEGINS TO SPIN OUT OF control. I develop a love for guns, hunting Crips, and fighting. I am becoming a man with needs impossible for my family to fulfill. Life is hard, money is tight, and I have to find a way to step up and get mine. My criminal mind works overtime as I become proficient at hustling and robbing.

After leaving Irvington, my next voyage begins on a rainy night, riding with my family down an unfamiliar block in Orange, New Jersey. I'm tired and Derrick is flowing to a rhyme by Redman. David is not with us.

Mom pulls into the backyard of a housing complex that's in terrible condition.

● ● ●

As the rain beats down on us, I help my mom and brother unload the U-Haul truck. We don't have much to unload, but the pouring rain drags the awful night out longer.

Once we finish, we begin arranging things in the house. I take a quick tour of my new residence that lasts no longer than fifteen seconds. The two-bedroom apartment is in a dingy-looking building. Clearly, the people who lived here before us didn't bother to clean before they left because we are welcomed by filthy underclothes and garbage.

We continue to unpack and rearrange the furniture for a couple of hours before calling it a night. Derrick and I will share a room and I don't like it. The room is small; we have to stack our clothes on top of other things.

At the end of the night, the three of us lay blankets on the hard living room floor, getting ready for bed. It feels like Buffalo in the winter, made worse by the fact that one of the living room windows is cracked. Mom says the heat will be on in a day or two, so until then we have to bear the conditions. She doesn't like it here either, but she always shows strength to let us know everything will be all right.

My stomach growls all night along with my brother's because we don't have anything to eat. As I toss and turn trying to get comfortable on the hard-ass floor, hundreds of ideas run through my head. I am extremely unhappy and I can't understand why Mama made us move again.

Getting ready to enter ninth grade reminds me of my third- and fifth-grade years. I have to start all over again. Everything in my life has been subject to drastic changes without so much as a sign or forewarning. I've always felt like a short-term guest everywhere I've been. Movement has been my companion, from house to house, room to room, neighborhood to neighborhood, street to street, school to school, and one pit to another.

An hour or so after we lie down, we hear banging on the front porch. *What the hell is that!* I jump up to look out the window. A bunch of teens are acting wild.

"I'll handle it, Mom." Mom shakes her head and says, "I'll call the police."

The group of thugs are getting louder and louder, busting bottles as if we aren't even inside. My hands tighten into fists. *My mother ain't gon' live in fear.*

I slip on my sneakers and go outside. On the porch are about ten guys shooting dice and drinking 40s. As I stare at them, it appears they are waiting for me to say something. I feel their eyes on me. Asking them to move off the porch will probably end in my getting my ass kicked. Weighing my options, I decide to turn around, close the door, and lie back down.

But I vow to myself to put an end to their game soon.


My first violent experience happens a month after moving in.

Ab has the bank as I prepare to roll the dice. I am on fire, because I have already taken him for about $400, and he has another stack on him. Ab is an ol' head on the block that moves major weight. He employs the young'stas to move his drugs. He rolls a 4, 5, 6 when Sleepy pulls up on a bike. Sleepy too is an ol' head who hustles on the block. He gets his name because he has to literally lift his head back just to see you. You can never tell if his eyes are open or closed.

"Who got bank?" Sleepy questions.

At this point, while in the middle of a sneeze that sends my attention up the street, I see a masked gunman sprinting directly toward us.

Boom, Boom, Boom, Boom!

Without delay, I find an escape to avoid the gunfire, as I realize that the attempt is for Ab.

Without hesitation, Ab drops the dice and breaks across the street, finding a way to escape the bullets that graze the wall.

Boom, Boom, Boom, Boom, Boom, Boom! Each shot that hits Sookie's Pub sends bits of the wall flying.

I find out that the shooter tried to kill Ab because Ab recently pistol-whipped him. However, days after the incident, the two of them are shooting dice, and drinking 40s together.

One full calendar year has gone by since I enrolled in Orange as a freshman. The year is passing by uneventfully, but soon that will all change.

My sophomore year, 1996, marks the year gang bangin' gets to Essex County, in particular Orange, New Jersey, my new home.

Sitting on my porch, I watch the elders rake in the dough. The 'hood I live in is one of the three most drug-infested communities in Orange.

Crackheads cram the block from sunup to sundown. I begin wanting some of that tax-free money. In my house, money isn't something we have much of. Mama works two full-time jobs just to pay the bills, and my stepfather, Norman, works for New Jersey transit. Despite his negative attitude toward me, he always pays the bills, and keeps food in the house. I avoid him as best I can. He doesn't like me, and shows me no affection. Sometimes when I speak to him, he ignores me. He's a bitter man and takes his frustrations out on my brother and me.

With the exception of playing football and basketball, I find companionship in the streets. I have all kinds of questions I want to talk to Mama about. But I can't, she's a woman, I'm a teenage boy, I need a man to talk to. Best believe there's nothing a teenager can't learn about in the streets. Sex, crime, drugs, sports, and politics. The 'hood is the local newspaper. I take all my problems to the streets. Mama is a strong Black woman, but she's no match for the streets. They embrace me in a way she can't. I get money from them, lessons about life, sex, and how to be a man.

I'm now sixteen years old. I don't want to wear the same clothes from last year. I want new clothes, money, things to impress the girls. I want to fit in.

I make up my mind and one day, seeing Rashawn sit on the sidewalk, I cop a squat next to him. He likes me because I look after his li'l cousin Mu. I explain to him my situation at home, and that I want in. He schools me right there on how to make money. He tosses me my first pack, a $100 clip of cocaine. Rashawn is respected on Day Street, and I look up to him. What I like most about him is he's low-key, just like me. Unless you know him, you will never guess he has tens of thousands of dollars from pushing cocaine.

I learn a lot by watching how Rashawn deals with people. He's a businessman. He treats the fiends fair, but he rules with an iron fist when they short him. When I start selling cocaine, I try to imitate his style. For a whole year, I watch him move drugs like clockwork. I know how to spot a crackhead a mile away. They have a walk only a hustler recognizes. I know all the fiends by first name, and all car sales by their honks. This, I find interesting. Car sales have specific honking patterns of three beeps, followed by a second pause, then two quick beeps. Rashawn set this up. It's the "I want to buy drugs" honk.

I move the pack Rashawn gives me in five minutes. *Damn, it's like that?* I head down the block to Rashawn with $100 for more drugs. I hand him $100 and he gives me five clips worth $500. He tells me I did a good job, and tells me to bring him back $200. Doing the math in my head, that means I profit $300. I like this deal. I sell five clips in thirty minutes. I have more money in my pocket than my mother. I feel good. I feel like a man.

After three days of stacking my money, my first order of business is to purchase my own gun. It's useless to gang bang and hustle, and not have a gun. Guns are to hustlers and bangers what cell phones are to moguls, just the accessories of doing business, you can't live without them.

Carrying guns does crazy things to my mind. The power I feel when I have one is irreplaceable. I look at life two ways. Either you can spare life or you can take life. When I carry a ratchet, I feel alive, powerful, and superior.

When I'm strapped, size doesn't matter. I don't care how big you are because my gun is stronger. Tough guys seem to lose their strength in my eyes. I know it's because of me that they still breathe, all because of my gun. That is power.

My love of guns is vindicated one night when I almost get robbed. Walking home from basketball practice around nine at night some Jurassic Park members and a nearby street gang I fight with spot and creep toward me. I feel the vibe that something fishy is about to happen. I stiffen and my antennas spring out.

I remove my .32 from my backpack. My fear of a potential attack disappears at the touch of the handle. I have the power. As they get nearer, I pull out the heat, aim, and bust off shots at them, Tat! Tat! Tat! In panic, they scatter, screaming. I watch them for a moment, soaking it all up. Then I turn and coolly flat-line home.


As a hustler the majority of my clientele comes from my pager. I sell drugs before, during, and after school. I often leave school to serve fiends on school property.

Mama has no clue I hustle because, for one, she's working two full-time jobs. However, one night, she catches me red-handed. I run down a car sell, and after making the transaction I stuff the money in my pocket and hold on to the remaining bottles. Standing on our porch, looking me square in my eyes, Mama says, "Boy what the hell was that?"

I know full well there is no way out of this and say, "Nothing Mom."

"Boy, don't play with me, I wasn't born yesterday. Did you just sell that man drugs? Get cho ass in the house before I break yo' neck. Are you fucking crazy? You gon' disrespect me and sell that shit in front of my house?"

Mama takes my new hustle harder than I thought. The fact is she had to know. She threatens to kick me out if I don't stop selling drugs. I, of course, agree with all her demands. However, once I step back outside, it's back to hustling. I move my business down the block, out of Mama's sight.

I met Saint my freshman year in high school. Our first encounter brought about a fight. Two bulls in one class, someone had to go.

During the winter break in 1996, Saint and Moody take a trip to Atlanta, Georgia. When they return, they come back Blood. It trips me out when I spot the two of them trooping through the halls with red flags hangin' from their back pockets. I approach them about the red. I have to know if what they're wearing signifies what I know it means.

My Phoenix days are a distant memory as far as bangin' goes because it's unheard of here. Saint's new way of life reintroduces gang life back into mine, and gives me something to look forward to. It rejuvenates me with the familiar something that is already rooted in me.

Saint embraces me as his brother, and we begin to assemble the Bloods in Essex County. In my mind, the wheels are turning. Feeding off the inspiration I get from movies like *Boyz in the Hood* and *Colors,* my appetite for gang life becomes insatiable. There's nothing like the brotherhood, especially when family is what you crave. Within the set we understand one another, fight for each other, and hold one another down. I miss the camaraderie. It's time for me to get back in the game. This time, I'm choosing my squad.

We begin recruiting those who are the same as us. We recruit from Orange, East Orange, Union, and Newark. Saint and I develop a tight bond. We don't allow harm to come among any of us.

I'm unmotivated, depressed, fatherless, without direction or guidance, but I feel love from my new family. We do everything together. Fight, protect, and fill voids that we can't get from home. If any of us got into some beef, we all banged out. We always mobbed in a group to prevent being attacked. And we listened to one another, talked, things that families are supposed to do.

One freezing winter night we have a meeting and one of the many topics discussed is how we feel about our fathers. There are fifteen of us drinking 40s and we all get extremely emotional with the help of the O-E. Until that day, I had never heard so much hate and pain as I did that night.

Saint and I both grew up without fathers, and learned at the hands of the streets all we needed to know to survive in them. Like me, he knows many nights of heating up his house by opening the oven door or putting water on the stove for a warm bath. Our wintertime heat came at the turn of a knob to 375 degrees.

Instead of only me being unmotivated, depressed, and fatherless, we *ALL* are. Here we are, fifteen and sixteen years old, suffering more mental and emotional pain than we can deal with. We all seem to welcome death as our destiny, whether in the ground or a jail cell. Gang bangin' will make that happen. The set is my clearest vision of strength. I soon begin to flip my entire world, revolving it around the gang.

Most of my homees' families are on drugs and live in the projects or other low-income housing. We vow to each other to be loyal or die.

In time, my mother begins intruding again in my personal life. Sensing the change in my attitude, she does what any normal mother would. She punishes me, and tells me what I can and can't do. What it really does is help incite me and create more distance in our relationship. Now I become crafty with her. I keep everything away from her. In my eyes, at this point, the parent becomes the enemy and must be avoided at all cost. Nothing is more important than my set.

Everything that goes on in my life, the gang is involved. This is what draws me closer to them. I can finally be with people whose Blood pumps the same way as mine. The homees take more interest in my life than my whole family. My mama, older brother, my stepfather, and certainly my father. My love for my homees begins to grow into a die-hard love.

Saint, Holiday, Jada, Haz, Sha Blood, and I head downtown to promote our affiliation. Since Blood is new to Essex County, we attract haters who don't respect Blood. Days earlier Sha Blood gets into a dispute with a broad in Li'l Bity where we hang after school. He's high when Shorty asked him for some smoke. He allows her to get it out of his pocket, but she takes the weed and $500. Today is the first time he's seen her since. Today the heat is cooking.

We all buy military knives from the army store on Market Street. Sha Blood sees home girl who beat him for his money. She's in front of the Chicken Shack with a group of guys. Sha Blood confronts her.

"Yo, where da fuck is my scrillah, bitch!"

She responds, "How the fuck would I know?"

"Stop lying bitch, I know you got my money, give dat shit up befo' it gets ugly out here on Blood!"

He throws a sign to Jada for an attack, which she carries out to perfection. Jada makes her move by striking the girl in the face with the knife, leaving her eye damn near hanging out of the socket. Jada follows with rapid punches while still poking.

We hear sirens in the distance, it's time to flat. As we all run in separate directions, Holiday and I make our way up Market Street. Saint and Haz get bagged, and Jada's caught running down Broad Street. Holiday and I jump on the bus hoping the rest will make it. Once Holiday and I make it back to my house, we impatiently wait for the others to arrive. Sha Blood finally makes it. He doesn't know what happened with Haz, Saint, or Jada. It turns out the police stationed Saint and Haz in the police booth on the corner of Broad and Market. Meanwhile, they are transporting Jada to the precinct to book her on the assault charge. She eventually gets sentenced three years for the crime.

The police decide to release Saint and Haz, though they should have known that the goons across the street, affiliates of home girl that just got half her face ripped off, want revenge. When Saint and Haz are released they are ambushed. Fifteen angry mothafuckas charge them like bulls. Saint and Haz brace themselves for the attack, are badly beaten, and left for dead. However, with no help by civilians, police, or EMTs, Saint makes it back to my house while Haz makes it back to Montclair.

Opening my front door, I'm shocked to see Saint.

"What the fuck Blood! What happened! Yo, come in, you need to get to the hospital!"

I barely recognize him. His face is twisted in all directions. I reach for him in an attempt to relieve him of the effort it will take to get upstairs. He's weak and dazed. He does his best to recall what happened, but falls asleep. Watching him sleep on my bed, I go into think mode. *We can't let this go slide. Dem niggaz gotta pay. We gotta send the message. They got my nigga all fucked up. Nah, man, nah, it ain't going down like dat on Blood.*

Once he wakes up, hours later, he explains what happened. I call a meeting with Face from 7 Deuce, his soldiers from New Community, and my soldiers. We rally for revenge. Can't stop, won't stop.

"Man, I'm riding on dem fools. I ain't beat Blood," Saint says. I can't let him take this ride. His condition is too severe to bang.

The vast weight of the mission falls heavily on my shoulders. It's incumbent upon me to destroy the persons involved, and keep the set on the winning end of all battles. At sixteen years old, this is a lot to deal with. I swear on the set to Saint, which is more religious to me than swearing to God: I'll see to it they feel the heat.

"Be bool Blood, be bool" is all I can say.

To which bro replies, "Yeah, 'cause I'm gonna make it right, watch."

I know in his heart he wants nothing more than to obliterate these fools' existence, but it's my call for him to stay behind. This is an opportunity to show him my love for him is thicker than water.

We hug briefly, as much as the soreness he feels will allow, and then Blood leaves without looking back. It's times like this when I hate my life most. Perhaps this is due to my not knowing answers to certain questions or being able to present my emotions on an intelligible level. So it's set for nighttime to get payback.

Darkness finally descends over the city and we make our way downtown. Face has the G-ride and Holiday mounts the plan. We park on a side block and flat-line to Broad and Market. As expected, they are out there at 12:00 A.M. hustling, straight slippin'.

Part one of Holiday's plans has us split up into three groups of two. Tonight, I'm dressed down in an all-Black mechanic's suit that I only wear for war and death. Heading into the crowd of would-be victims, I wonder if they'll recognize me from earlier. I take post under the bus stop while Face and Holiday engage in a conversation. The other two homees are on cell phones pretending to call a cab. Once Holiday gives the cry "Sooo Wooop," our sign to ambush them, we begin. Gunplay was our first option but we choose a more brutal attack. Knifing and poking sends a more emotional message. It's a different mind-set to complete this tactic. Cutting the flesh is more exhilarating to me than shooting.

Holiday disappears from my sight while we wait for the signal to move. Before we get it, Holiday makes his move without us. Now in full attack mode, I retrieve the handheld bat and shank I have tucked under my suit. I swing the bat, first connecting to the side of enemy number one's head. Barry Bonds ain't have shit on me tonight. As I make my attempt to shank this fool, I hear "Shoot 'em!" from one of his comrades. As I retreat, Face is cornering one of them while Holiday is attacking with a 2x4. Once I realize they have no gun, I continue my attack. I bang homee up again. I finished him off with a grand slam. Whack!

The shot is so perfect, he can't scream as consciousness is clearly lost.

I make my way toward Holiday to assist him in his attack. Face shouts "F-L Blood." Not wanting to adhere completely to the order to leave, I swing my bat once more with all my energy, hitting my victim in his torso. Immediately afterward, we regroup and make our escape. Job well done.

We assume there will be retaliation. We head back to New Community. Instead of heading home, I opt to stand on guard for any retaliation. We hide in our respective hideouts waiting and waiting.

From a distance of about twenty feet Holiday whispers to me, "That's dem Blood."

A car making its way onto Hayes Street is our expected target. Face says, "Shoot it, shoot it."

I raise my 9mm as I begin walking toward the car, gun fully extended. As I step closer to the car, I can see it's a woman driving and what looks to be a small child in the front seat. It's about 2:30 A.M. now and we are liquored up. As I get inches from the car, my suspicions are confirmed. I'm right, an elderly lady with a small child eight or nine years old. The look they give me as they stare down the barrel of my 9mm throws me off for a minute. Immediately I tuck the slammer in my waist and make my way back to my hideout.

Now pushing 3:30 A.M., I decide to catch a cab home.

When I get home, I call and tell Saint about our successful maneuver. He's satisfied. Our attack leaves two of the four enemies scarred for life.


Back at school weeks have passed, and things are looking up. I have become popular with the ladies. The fellas respect me. Saint and I turn the heat up in school as far as Blood goes. There are a few incidents that test us. There's unfinished beef between the Bloods and Jurassic Park.

On North Day Street pushing drugs, my phone rings. It's Saint.

"Dez Jurassic pussies came to my chick's house earlier trying to fight." I instantly get heated and ready to put work in.

"Yo Blood, dem niggaz try'na fade Blood." By now his anger has grown to an animated outburst.

"Be easy homez, we gon' take care of dat shit. I'm a round the soldiers up, man we 'bout to get down wit da get down."

"Nah Blood, dem lames ain't strong enough for that. We got 'em tomorrow Blood, you feel me Blood?"

By now I've already mounted an attack in my head only to be brought back to reality with his decision to wait.

"Yeah . . . yeah . . . I hear you Blood. Next day homee Sooo Woop!"

At 7:30 the following morning Saint, Moody, and I confront ten of them in the cafeteria. We are all cherried up, ready for a brawl. I demand their attention with my B-Boy posture.

"Who got the fuckin' problem with my homee? Y'all came to his shorty's brib on some fighting shit?"

Phil is the shot-caller for Jurassic Park. He and I have a mutual respect for each other's position within our respective crews.

No one responds to my claims so I scream, "What's bangin' Blood?"

By now Phil feels compelled to say something. "Dae hold up, they—"

Saint cuts Phil off. "Yeah, you fag. Wass bang'n nigga?" He stares down his adversary, Malik, who started this beef.

Malik finally speaks. "We can take this out back," with as little confidence as an amateur about to fight Mike Tyson.

As both sides head out the back door, I notice we are outnumbered.

Considering the respect Phil has for me, I don't believe they'll jump us. I take my chances anyway.

Once outside, I feel confident Saint will win the man-to-man battle, but if he starts to lose, I'll intervene and that's when all hell will break loose.

Saint ties his red flag around his knuckles and throws up Piru with his fingers. He throws the setup and squares toe-to-toe with Malik. I know immediately after they begin fighting that Malik doesn't wanna bang. His camp continues to hype him up. Most suckas do this: allow their team to soup them up and then get beat the fuck up.

Saint's punches come in rapid succession. His opponent's defense is destabilized by each wallop.

Saint dominates the fight while I keep close watch on his challenger's entourage. It's clear to me they want to interfere with the fight but, considering their opponents, elect not to.

The fight ends with one last blow by Saint to Malik's chin. I jump in and stop the thrashing. Saint wants more.

"Blood don't want no mo'," I say trying to convince him to calm down. From that day on, Blood is definitely in the building, and is out for respect. The word Blood is held sacred to us. We enjoy calling each other Blood, and Blood bouncing.

# DRASTIC MEASURES

*Side of the tracks that was wrong*
*Left I was to roam*
*Cat of the alley I am*
*Feast of another man's garbage I must*
*For a cat's heart won't escape this dog's pain*
*A pain someone's love can cure*
*For God's plan is now a devil curse*
*A pig was its skin to now only be a dream*
*A dream not to be eaten*
*Wonder I do if mommy still sees her mirror reflection*
*Image of an empty baby bottle reflects my pain*
*For a bag of fills the holes in my left souls*
*Fear is produce from flesh surrounding steel*
*For no brother of mine will go hungry call nightfall*

HUSTLING AND FIGHTING WERE NOT MY ONLY TALENTS. WHILE still in high school, I became skilled at robbing fools. It seems like this time in my life was spent progressing from one type of crime to another. I was power-hungry and loving the very act of every score.

• • •

July 4, 1997, was a warm, typical day in Orange. The temperature was in the 80s, with a clear blue sky. I'm on Shaddy, which is how we refer to Day Street because the homees on the block are shaddy individuals. Shooting the breeze with Meggette, he begins a heated conversation about jacking a cop's crib in the neighborhood.

His passion for such a risky move is caused by his need for money. He hustles with me but isn't as dedicated as I am. He has something better in mind. He's on the verge of being evicted with nowhere to live. I sensed a few times, when I would finish selling my coke before him, that he didn't want me to leave. It's depressing to go into his house, stepping over piles of clothes and junk everywhere. He does his best to provide for his mother and younger brother.

So, I can't help but entertain the topic of his power move. I have the same problems and anything that can get me a quick buck is owed my attention. He's slow to tell me about his plan. He knows I'll decline if it doesn't add up. He purposely takes longer pulls of the sticky green before telling me. The plan sounds too easy and too risky at the same time. I mean, if we can escape the trap of getting through phases one and two of this crib, the rest will be a cakewalk. But it's the first two steps that I don't feel comfortable with.

"Yo Dae, this is a piece of cake man I'm telling you, I got it all mapped out."

With a deep sigh I reply, "Man you brazy homez?" He studies me, searching for the smirk that often crosses my face after a potential jux, robbery. Juxes come anytime we see an opportunity to gain some money, jewelry, clothes, or food. After a few moments of cautious contemplation, examining the angles of the plan, Meg asks, "So iz you in or what Blood?" When I refuse to take part, he is momentarily speechless with indignation.

I tried to persuade him of the risks. "I know that mothafucka got all types of security, shit we probably don't even know about."

"I doubt it. Check it out, I stole a stun gun from this White boy in West Orange a few days ago, and that will take out dem punk-ass dogs."

At this point, I think he's been served angel dust instead of regular weed. I begin laughing. "Yo, get cho Rambo ass outta here." I can't take him seriously at that moment since he is loaded with weed and Henny. But his posture and assertiveness suggested he means everything he's saying. I picture him crawling through the backyard with mud all over his face, shotgun shells hanging around his neck, and shouting "Cover me." I can't believe what he's telling me. Stun guns, ripping off cops, and dismantling security systems seem like an episode of the television show *MacGyver*. It seems like with every pull he inhales and slowly exhales, the more bizarre his plan gets. It starts out as just a robbery. Then he jacks someone for a tranquilizer gun. Next, we break into the house, shoot the dogs, and dismantle the security alarm. So far, at this point, I think homez is really tweaking. Our jackings have only consisted of sticking dealers, gas stations, pizza and Chinese delivery, and other small things throughout the 'hood. I think homee has really outdone himself this time.

Eventually I start to favor this plan because in all actuality, the dogs are my biggest concern. Even though the whole plan sounds chancy, he does have a solution to my biggest concern. The cop has three Doberman pinschers that I'm sure are highly trained to tear the balls off dumb-ass niggas like us. You know the kind that has ears that stand at attention and foamy drool at the mouth. But I am still reluctant to say I'm in. I know it irritates him because I don't fall in line with his plan right away.

"I'm saying, Meg, even if we get past the dogs, we still have to dismantle the security alarm. We don't know shit about that." To my surprise, Meggette has been dealing with this cat from East-wick, in Elizabeth, New Jersey, that can break into the White House if he has the proper comrades. As Meggette blows clouds of smoke off into the distance, I spot a vehicle on the corner of Gist and Day Streets.

I wave my hand in front of Meg's face to get his attention before saying, "Yo Meg, you B that car ova dere?" I nod my head in the direction of the unmarked car while squinting my eyes for a better look.

"Where?" he says.

"Right dere nigga look!"

Nothing out of the ordinary registers to me. We both step into the light for the car to see us. The car then begins to make its way in our direction as I say to Meg, "B, you married?"

"Nah my strap in da back."

"Five-0 ran down before you came out, and I know dem fools coming back."

Usually when individuals on the turf are not strapped, it gives more meaning to the saying "It's better to get caught with it, than without it." The closer the car gets, the more nervous I become, but I still can't identify it. At this point, I am more afraid it is the police as opposed to an enemy.

The car comes to a complete stop across the street in front of Sookie's Pub. The driver's side window slowly rolls down as a voice follows. "Y'all got wholesale?"

I look at the face of the driver, I assume he's a hustler, and it puts me at ease. I look at Meg with a questioning face, You think they police? But he looks back at me with the same face. So I shout back, "What chu want?"

Meggette in a low voice says to me.

"You know dem?"

"Hell nah."

The driver and the passenger discuss what they want, and the driver shouts back, "Onion."

We just reupped the day before, so we have plenty. I go to the back of the building where the stash spots are, pull out an ounce and fill a Ziploc bag with a rock. When I return to the street, the two occupants have exited their car and are making small talk with Meggette. At this point I figure, shit, another day another dollar. While serving the driver, his man is burning flames in the side of my head with his stares. I play it cool and go through the transaction like I don't notice him. Meg and I are both unarmed. We are already slipping, I tell myself.

*I know this cat from somewhere.* He looks familiar and since his fitted is covering his beady eyes, I can't place the questionable face to any particular place. This bothers me more than anything because I don't know if I am standing before a potential enemy.

After the deal is done, they head back to their car.

As they pull off, I ask Meg, "Blood, you recognize Blood wit' da hat?"

He shakes his head from left to right while licking his thumb rearranging his money.

Beep, Beep, Beep, my pager goes off. It's Holiday. I flat-line over to the 'hood's pay phone. I throw a dime in the phone, punch in some numbers, and wait to hear his voice.

"What it ru," Holiday sounds off.

"Shit, booling on da block. You boming through?"

"Not tonight Blood. I gotta head out to da Bity."

"Wait, wait a minute," I cut in before he hangs up.

"Yo, you want me to meet chu out there?"

Before I can hear his response, Meggette yells, "Brabbz!"

Turning abruptly on the drive-by, I am just in time to catch a glimpse of the first spark of the gun. Suddenly, the ear-splitting shots! Boc, Boc, Boc, echoes throughout the bottom of Day Street while bullets whistle by me. It's second nature to drop the phone and hit the deck. I manage to maneuver, ducking and sprinting to the alley. For several seconds afterward, I hear nothing but ringing in my ears. The shooter is definitely not a good shooter because I had my back to the streets.

After retreating to the back of my building, I scoop up the sawed-off, and run back to the block looking for the Crabs. Meggette comes out from the other side with his chopper. We check to make sure neither of us is hit, and try to figure out if we know who the shooters are. I'm still in shock. *These mothafuckas really tried to put holes in me.*

"It was dem fools we just served a li'l while ago," Meggette informs. "Blood, dat nigga hung out the window with a flue rag over his face. I saw dem mothafuckas at the last minute, but they couldn't see me because I was in the cut."

Bingo, it all registered to me who they were. Crips! Two weeks ago, Holiday and I had gotten into a beef with some Crabs downtown. It only went as far as us spitting out razors before the police stopped the beef.

The shooter is the same fool who was calling us slobs.


One night, soon after escaping this situation, I'm trippin' on the fact that I almost got smoked. Living my violent lifestyle, there is no rest for the weary. Even in the privacy and supposed comfort of my home, I have no peace of mind. My mind is battle-scarred and there's so much at stake—my life, my money, and my sanity—always threatened to be taken from me. My days and nights are filled with all-consuming worries about bangin' and surviving. And facing the reality that I just barely cheated death has got me on edge.

Standing at my bedroom window watching the clouds cover the sky, I touch the glass and think about death. For most of my life, the line separating life from death has been as thin as the window on which my fingers rest. It's like that when you know people are trying to kill you.

There is a knock at my door. I spin, quick as a snake, hand reaching for my gun.

"Dinner's ready," Mama says behind the door. I relax.

"Be there in a minute." I turn back to the window.

*I deserve a better life than this. We never should have moved here.*

Later that night, I'm sitting downstairs laughing as I watch *Martin*. When the show is over, I head upstairs to take a shower. As I make my way past the last step, I hear Mama crying in her room. Leaning in closer to the door, I can hear her crying and praying to God. Just an hour ago, she was sitting at the kitchen table paying bills. This is routine. Mama always gets depressed when the bills come. She wears this look on her face that says, "This is what my life is about, working to pay bills." Her sadness affects me too. It makes me feel useless.

*I have to find a way to contribute.*

I need a way to get more money of my own. My plan is to start jacking. I'll help Mama out by sticking people up.

The next morning I enter the shower, letting cold water spray over my head and down my back, hoping to ease my tension and frustration.

My shower lasts ten minutes, but doesn't do anything to ease my stress. After throwing on my Black Dickies suit I step onto the block. It's hot as hell, which doesn't help. My mind is looking for something to get into to release my anger.

Chinese food, I think, as my mouth begins to water. I head to the pay phone, throw a dime in, and wait to hear the strongly accented Chinese man.

"Take out or deliver?"

"Delivery."

I make a note to order somewhere around $50 worth of food. I tell the guy that I have a $100, so I'm sure he'll bring change. Once the order is complete, I go back into the house, retrieve my .380, and wait patiently for my food.

The entire time I wait, I mentally beat myself up. I think of all the shit my family and I are dealing with. I justify my actions as a result of my mother's misfortunes.

Thirty-five minutes later, a white Geo pulls up, and a short man gets out of the car with the food.

"Forty-two dollars and fifty cents," he says.

*Stupid mothafucka,* I think as I pull out and cock my .380. "Give me the fucking money before I bust a cap in yo' ass!" He responds promptly, dropping the bag with a hysterical look on his face. His body freezes up and he doesn't move. I snatch the money and wallet from his pockets. Flipping through, I see he's a family man, with three kids, all boys.

I order him to run up the block, and if he stops, he's dead. He's still in shock, and motionless, so I clobber him over the head with the butt of the gun. "Run mothafucka!" As he runs up the street, I run down the street. I head to Meggette's house. We split $250, and fill our stomachs with wings and fries. Another successful night of work.

I learn how to rob from my godbrother Roc. When I say rob, I mean the craft involved in the actual act. When Meg and I first start out, we would pull out our guns ordering, "Give it up!" By the time I learn all I need from Roc I can mentally rob someone without saying anything at all. It's the complete control, mentally and physically, that I love. A fool being absolutely submissive to my every demand. I have the power.

Roc teaches me the strong-armed jack move. Sometimes Erick

and I will practice and other times Meggette and Erick. It's a two-man technique. I will clip the legs of the vic while Meggette or Erick holds him at gunpoint. If done right you keep a small distance between yourself and the vic, who may try to be a superhero and grab you. While Meg has the gun aimed at the vic, I instruct the vic to empty his pockets and remove everything: money, jewelry, wallet. Afterward, we turn and run like the wind. This move is only done to people who are by themselves and who look flashy. We are the reason people use the buddy system at night on the streets.

Jackings give me a rush unlike selling drugs. The biggest difference is that it's less time-consuming especially when you factor in all the hours standing around, chasing cars, and running from the police that dealing involves. There's an adrenaline rush when I whip my burner out. It's a confidence-booster to see how the toughest guys cry for their lives when I cock that shit back.

One night, we stick up a group on a corner that is known for having big banks in the Valley. As they stand under a streetlight rolling dice, we walk up, me, Meggette, and Erick, whip out three guns, forty-eight rounds, and strip them down to their boxers. We take their clothes, shoes, jackets, and jewelry. The windchill has to be in the teens, and just for kicks, I order them to remove their boxers and lie on the ground face first. We split $1,500, pawn the jewelry, and keep the jackets.

Jacking almost costs me one of my prized possessions. Meggette, Derrick, Sho, Saint, and I are leaving downtown Newark in a cab. On the ride back, Saint and Sho are chopping it up about some broad while I zone off into space. Crossing Park Avenue, a big knot of crispy twenties in the ashtray catches my attention. My excitement must've tipped the cabbie off because not one second afterward, he discreetly closes the tray.

I sit in the front seat while the rest occupy the back. It's somewhere around three or four in the afternoon. *I gotta jack this fool.*

I throw up a sign indicating a 311, which is robbery. I now redirect our drop-off location from in front of my house to a side block in my 'hood, Gist Place, which is adjacent to Day Street.

As the car comes to a stop, I already have the gun locked and loaded in my right hand. I jam the barrel of the hammer to the side of his cheek, while Saint puts him in a choke hold to secure him. I grab the stash out of the ashtray, and by now all three doors are swinging open simultaneously. We all scamper down Gist, to the back of my building. As we run, I hear the cabdriver screaming for help.

While running, I place the gun in the front of my pants as we all sprint up the stairs. I suddenly hear, Pop! The gun goes off in my pants and momentarily paralyzes me. I had forgotten to uncock the .38 once I got out of the cab. I pause in a frantic shock, not wanting to believe I could have possibly done the unthinkable. For a full minute, the world stands still. Everybody, including me, is too scared to look and afraid to speak. Heart still pounding, I begin slowly unbuttoning my pants to take a look before noticing that the bullet went through my pants, leaving a full-blown hole in them.

Saint says in a concerned voice, "Yo Blood, did you shoot ya self?"

"I—I—"

I can't formulate the words in order to give him a response. The gun spark leaves a burning sensation that pales in comparison to the merriment that follows. These fools are laughing!

Days later Meg and I plan to jack another cab. We call a cab from a pay phone and have it pull up on Elizabeth Street. I check the .38 revolver to make sure all six shots are there but realize there are only four left. We used two bullets earlier shooting out streetlights.

We did this every so often to keep the 'hood as dark as possible.

Once the cab pulls up on Elizabeth, Meg and I nonchalantly walk up to it holding a conversation. Meg enters the backseat first. I follow. It's well past midnight, so we don't wear masks. However, we both have on low-fitted hats. There's a woman accompanying the driver in the passenger's seat. At this point, Meg and I eye each other indicating the go-ahead. With the hammer already in hand, Meg puts the ratchet against the back of the driver's head. I gather the woman is probably his wife. As we demand the money, the cabbie says "No" in a strong Haitian accent. The woman begins screaming uncontrollably. Meg cracks both of them in the back of their heads as we decide to flee. Sometimes our plans didn't always work out.

At this point in my life, my appetite for the street life is insatiable. It seems like every time I turn around I'm a player in some back-to-back nonsense. Eventually, all my wildin' and the burden it put on my mind starts to become too much to ignore. Then one day, my mind starts trippin'.

I go into the bathroom and stand in front of the sink, gazing into the mirror. I turn on the faucet. I wash my hands—bend over, splash water onto my face. When I rise, face dripping, about to reach for a towel, I catch sight of a shadowy figure standing in the mirror watching me. Startled, I yelp, stumble backward, slip, and fall to the floor. Breathing hard, I look around the bathroom. I'm alone, of course. Heart knocking, I look up at the mirror. I can't see the full view of the mirror from where I'm sitting. What the hell is that? I grasp the front of the sink. Groaning, I pull myself to my feet, checking the mirror again. I see only my damp face. No one else. It's my imagination, I reason. What's the matter with me? Something horrible is happening.

# BLOOD'N

*Souls that cry to lose*
*Pain can only be felt if I'm dying for less*
*Bounded by a color that severed me from my brother*
*Wishing no longer to live*
*Death is only to embrace*
*Dreams are not to dream*
*For I have not awakened from my hell*
*Believe I do in death*
*For I have not seemed to live*
*Eyes behold scars only my soul shall hold*
*Closed eyes express my death*
*For my only light was a flag of red*
*Sad I had to be for I knew it would be the death of me*

I AM A GENERAL. I COMMAND SCORES OF SOLDIERS WHO ARE committed to riding and dying for the set. As a leader I must always have the brilliant plan, rally the troops, and be ready to hit the battlefield at a moment's notice. *With these skills I could be anything I want to be—a professional athlete, a doctor, a businessman, whatever. But right now, I am just a ghetto genius—will I ever be more?* On the turf, shit constantly happens; gang banging clouds your judgment and it's all-consuming.

I've managed to make it to my eighteenth birthday. I'm the captain of the football team and a full-time gang banger. I allow both elements to operate in tandem as I excel in both.

Today is an ordinary day, cloudy and a bit nippy. Gearing up, I take extra precaution to dress warm. The set agrees to meet on Shady Ville at 10:00 P.M., which is our headquarters. I'm dressed in my Black Air Force Ones with phat red laces, Black army pants, and a Black sweater. I just got my hair braided in box braids a few days before, and over these I wear a burgundy flag in bangin' fashion.

Riding around Dodd Town in East Orange Crip huntin' is a night to remember. Like déjà vu all over again, we get into our zones, asking within for the strength to perform at our best. It doesn't take long before the Cisco kicks in.

We pack in one of the home girl's car, Tiffany's MPV, to set out for some Blood loving and purification of our flags. It's Meggette, Saint, Snipe, Face, E, Bo, and me on the hunt.

Once we get to Dodd Town, we ride around looking for the prey before spotting a group of guys huddled around a car. I tell Tiffany to circle the block, and pull up alongside them so we can blast them. It's five of them and two females in the car from what I can see. Dodd Town is known for Crip activity, so anything in blue is an immediate target. As we drive past these guys, they seem to all be dressed down in blue, or so I think. The mission is to eliminate anything breathing, Operation Paint the Town Red.

Exiting the van, I hear the beautiful sound of Meggette and his pump becoming one. He fills the stomach of his weapon with thug food that will give these Rickets something to be sick about.

I form my fingers into a P, and kiss them with passion to the heavenly skies. Approaching the car of soon-to-be casualties of war, I shout, "Funk!" The next thing I hear is something a rider never wants to hear at a time like this.

"Dashaun!" in a high feminine voice. Damn did that still the high I have and need.

I immediately shout "En Vogue," commanding my troops to fall back. Saint is mumbling something to himself to the effect of "fuck dem." The unsuspecting delay irritates him because he has already pictured how we'd leave them.

*How the fuck could someone recognize me with my flag over my face, and skully on my head?* I need to find out who is this mystery person that knows me. It turns out that it isn't my appearance that gives me away, but my voice.

The female, who in the midst of my purification shouts, not my alias, but government name, is a girl named Angel from my high school. She is my cheerleader for the football team. All the starters on the team have personal cheerleaders who shout cheers for that individual player. They also wear our jerseys game day and during school. Angel is one of the two cheerleaders assigned to me, captain and quarterback of the football team. Over-whelmed with the fact that she is present during our happy hour, we retreat back to our vehicle. As for the individuals waiting to be executed, the expressions on their faces suggest they aren't ready to die. They are shaking, and begging for their lives without speaking.

I walk back to the sidewalk and call Angel over.

"What the fuck you doin' out here! You don't even live out here, you know where the hell you at?"

Unaware of the neighborhood she's in she replies, "No I don't know this area, but they ain't Crips Dae, I know them."

"You sure they ain't Rickets Angel? Don't fuck wit me!"

"Hell no! I wouldn't lie to you, for real Dae."

I don't know if I'm more upset that she said my name or the fact that we didn't complete our mission.

"Get the hell outta da streets because it's a war zone out here."

She timidly hugs me and whispers in my ear, "Please B safe Dae."

"Trillz, I got this," pointing to my heater, "you bee this, I'm a B aright. Go home Angel."

*Driving away from Angel, I think to myself, If she wasn't there, a few more Rickets would have bit the dust. Luckily for her, she recognized my voice or she would have been capped up too.* How would I have felt reading it in the papers, that a group of unknown non-gang members were brutally murdered along with my home girl Angel?

The homees and I get back in the van and speed off, but then I start wondering would she tell what she witnessed.


It was now at the point where we would be in gunfights several times a week. One day we heard that the Hoover Crips tried to fade two of my homees.

Once I get word, Ace, Saint, Derrick, Buggz, Face, Murder, and I are ready. We have two cars as we mob through their 'hood. Upon arriving on their set, I check to make sure my clip is full. I remove my red flag from my right pocket and tie it over my face, bangin' fashion.

Creeping slowly down Columbia Street, I keep a watchful eye for possible Crip patrols or shooters who might signal our being there and blow our surprise attack. And, of course, the likelihood if we don't strike without delay, that they will mount a comeback and box us in.

I was never fond of playing a block all day. Especially when you are gang banging, you leave yourself exposed for easy pickings. Twenty homees crammed on one block is about as dumb and obvious as fat kids hiding behind skinny trees playing manhunt.

We leave our vehicles to get more intimate with these 5 deuce Hoovers who we hate. Four of them post up on the porch while three more are on the sidewalk. Two of them are Crip walking, and the sight of it turns my stomach. *I hope y'all enjoy ya funny dance 'cause it's the last one you'll be doing.*

We shout gang disses, "CK nigga, fuck Hookers, Piru gang bang."

I catch one of them speed-walking to the side of the house where I know they keep their shooters. As he tries to make a run for his weapon, I step closer in the street, shout, "Funk!"

Boc, Boc, Boc! I launch seven more rounds at the scattering Hookers. The gate in front of the house catches three of them. Poor li'l Crabs never had a chance to claw their way out.

Bangin' equals revenge. I breathe this. I eat this. I'm a Blood.

I always save at least one bullet to secure our getaway. I know we don't have enough firepower to sustain a potential shootout.

So Ace, Derrick, and I jump back in Ace's G-ride, while two other homees take off on foot, leaving the last homee to shake the spot solo in his ride. I've wounded four Crips in total. Once out of the vicinity of Crip 'hood, we stop to dump the piece.

We all meet back up at Pooh's house. Satisfied with the work put in for the set, we do our gangsta shakes, hugs, and pay homage to the 'hood with our gangsta hops.

The next morning, I awake from a nightmare about the previous night's shooting. Only now I am on the other end of the gun getting sprayed up.

These are the moments when I am reminded that I'm trapped in a living nightmare. A personal hell filled with the suffering I continually cause others. As crazy as this cycle is, it is my life—a spinning wheel that routinely lands on danger and death. It's like a cruel twist on the old rhyme rewritten just for me, "round and round it goes, and where it will stop, we already know."

A few weeks after the ride on the Hoovers, I get a phone call from Mu Ru, "We back at it." We have just labeled Main Street Mafia Crips, who we refer to as Main Squeeze Mushys, as our newest enemies. We have to strike. They're growing in our neigh-borhood; we don't want them there. Tonight's ride will prove our love for our set and reinforce our territory. The plan is in place—Operation Seek and Destroy.

At 10:00 P.M. sharp everyone arrives at Saint's house. We go into our last-minute preparations before entering combat. We rally, go over our plans. I polish and examine my gun for any signs of malfunctions.

Mu Ru, an active YG, young gangster, always zones off when it's time for war. He's in a world of his own. I love him. He shoots me his most gangster look. "We ride together, we die together." He's a gangster, he's on Blood business. The liquor we drank already performs its duty on Mu. He says, "I love you Blood, we gon' ride tonight. Fuck dese Main squeezes let's ride," while ban-gin' two big Ps on his chest.

"Funk love . . . Blood," I add. At the same time we connect Ls as a sign of pure uninterrupted gangsta love. This is how we act when it's time to ride, proving our loyalty to each other. No one is guaranteed to come back alive.

There is nothing more satisfying than being with your homees loaded with alcohol and guns, knowing they will die for you. This is power. I have the power to either kill someone or let them live.

Tonight, I've sewn three Black bandannas together. I wear Black from head to toe. This is a ritual: I wear what I wanna die in. I check myself in the bathroom mirror. I'm flamed up, down fo' da 'hood. With two Ps on both hands, I salute myself. Banging teaches me to go against everything life has intended.

What's weird to me is that I always recite a prayer to the heavens, as if I want backup to help me against the enemy. I don't believe in God, but if one does exist, he can help me now.

The prayer goes like this:

"Almighty, I come before you in need of strength many say only you can provide. The strength that I speak of is that for destruction, with no regard for the enemy's life. Please watch over me and my set as we enter the battlefield." I memorized this prayer so thoroughly I can recite it backward.

The last few moments of the sun's rays are falling on the streets of Newark. While most of the working class is settling down, preparing for bed or a late-night movie, for the citizens of the streets, the night belongs to us.

We head into enemy territory. Our intelligence informs us of enemy sightings on Stuyvesant Avenue. I pack into the G-ride, fully loaded, stoned outta my mind, with stone-cold riders. We take the back streets of the city heading into our enemy's territory, all the time scoping out for squad cars.

Saint's music in the car amps me up more. *"They say killers never prosper I can't tell if being real was a sin I wouldn't see you in hell."* I bop my head to the beat, soaking up every lyric. As I rap in chorus, I wave my gun around in the air.

*"The tech's the storm bullets dripping eating through ya flesh."* I reset the CD and start rapping all over again. *"War, what is it good for, poppin niggas' tops,"* I shout with my eyes closed, trying to space out. I get more and more whacked each time I play the song. I repeat the song at least five times. *"War, it relieves my stress catch 'em slippin' leave 'em bleedin' till it ain't nothin' left!"* I shout, "Turn right here Blood!" at T. Dot. *"No guts, you a mutt to dese streets, put chu to sleep."*

Upon arrival, all safeties are released and last-minute signs and hugs are given.

I'm ready. I think about the possibility of this being my last ride. *"I love you Blood,"* I manage to say to Mu Ru through the tears.

*"I love you more Blood,"* he says. *"Let's put that funk down on dese squeezes."*

Scanning our attack location, our eyes meet, Enemy! Enemy! Enemy! My inner voice howls. Five Brabs are bick'n'it on the porch doing their Crab shit. Reassuring myself one last time that my strap is ready to spit, I cock it back, moved by the lovely sound. Click! Clack! Circling around, we ride around the enemy's 'hood a few times, waiting to catch them at their most vulnerable state.

Just like every other time, my conscience starts screaming. *Maybe I shouldn't, what if we get caught. No time for that shit now!* Eventually the guilt passes. It gets easier the more you do it. But they are in violation by default. They're Crips, I'm Blood. They see me, they kill me; I see them, I kill them. I am ready to die but not on the enemy's watch. This is war, this is Blood'n. Everyone has a responsibility to represent for the set. We must fight the Crips at a moment's notice. We attack by drive-bys or doing walk-ups.

Everyone in the car is calm as we prepare for the ambush. I grab hold of the 151, tilt it to my lips, and gulp away. "Agghhh," I growl as the liquor drips down my throat burning along the way. I hate the taste of liquor, but tonight I love it. I wait for it to travel to my brain and deaden all the frustration inside me. I let tears out, fighting back the current that hides behind my eyes. I sit hunched and whacked outta my mind, until the distraction of guns being chambered demands my attention.

The streets are silent. The only sound is cocking hammers. My mind is completely shut down. My heart beats faster and faster. My only thoughts are about death.

It's hot enough to fry bacon on the streets, for the cops are on patrol for gang activity. There's only split-time intervals for an attack to be carried out. If not in and out within matters of seconds, 5–0 will surely be in pursuit. We pull the car up to our designated location and kill the lights. Bullets are wiped clean, removing all fingerprints. Stacking my name and 'hood on my fingers, I pump up the Machete aspect of my personality. At this point, I'm empowered. I'm addicted. I'm on Blood business. One reckless car, fully equipped: four shooters, three experienced, and over fifty rounds of ammunition equals one Bloody mess.

Exiting the G-ride, we scream everything under the sun. P'z up! Funk Brabbz! Ru gang! CK nigga! I realize how calculated my train of thought is; I have rehearsed in my mind, preparing myself for the mission. My brain is in overdrive, but I still remain calm under such nerve-racking conditions. I count five Crips on the porch, and one I later find out is a Cripette. Don't matter though; we are making a blockbuster movie.

Boom! Boom! I fire again as the remaining targets run in all directions, desperately trying to avoid slugs meant to erase them. Snack and Mu are exercising their trigger fingers as T. Dot shoots across my face from the driver's seat. I can feel the recoil on the side of my face after each shot he fires. I shout, "Fuck Crabs, SWOOP GANG!" We peel out leaving the scene Bloody. My gun is smoking like a chimney. It's odd to me they'd be off guard because we just exchanged bullets with them days earlier. Nonetheless, we take pride in catching them slippin'. Following the attack, we slide back into the G-ride and murk off.

Tat! Tat! Tat! The Crips shoot back at us. Luckily for us, no one is hit, but every inch of me wants to turn around and serve them again. Our tires spin and screech as we shake the spot. We hand the burners off to Murder and Face, who are stationed three blocks away. We head back to headquarters. Afterward, instead of grief and repentance, we exult in hugs, brews, and gang signs. And yet, my attitude toward my enemy is just a mere reflection of what I feel inside—suicidal. I don't care if I live or die.

Two weeks later, riding with my homee B-Brim from Brick City Brim, I have a run-in with my past. B-Brim is a Blood I hook up with every now and then when I need a ride or an emergency gat. He's always down to gang bang with me, but he's definitely a family man. That's what I like about him so much; he's also a gentleman. We stop at a red light and I meet the eyes of the fool in the blue Monte Carlo at the crossing light. His name is Loc'sta. I just shot at him three weeks earlier. I know this Crip from middle school. He instantly recognizes me as it seems like he gets excited. It's around five or six in the afternoon because the sun has not set. He's in the passenger seat with a blue rag around his neck. I'm almost certain he's strapped and probably out looking to hunt some Bloods. I have my .380 on my lap and I think about letting off at the light. Considering the amount of traffic, I decide on waiting. As the light turns green and we pull off, the car he's in pulls behind another car as they discreetly follow us. As soon as I spot the tail, I figure this situation will end in gunfire. "B, pull over; I'm a blast 'em." I know B-Brim's down but a little reluctant because he's in his family car. Doing dirt in your primary whip ain't cool, especially if it's the one your wife and mother drive. Sometimes it is what it is though. By now, we are crossing over Springfield Avenue with the one car separating them from us. The back of my head is getting warm; I can be shot in the back of the head. I keep a close eye on them from the rearview mirror but I'm anxious knowing there are bullets behind me. B-Brim slides down a bit in his seat because his head damn near touches the roof of the car.

I don't know why cats always do this, and I am a victim of it myself. I eject the magazine just to check to make sure I am full, knowing damn well I am. I guess it's somewhat comforting to hear that Click! Clack! This sound brings you back to reality, snaps you out of it, and commands your attention. However, by the time we reach Clinton Avenue, for some reason they bust a right onto Clinton, and lucky for them—or us—it's the right decision.

# FINAL DESTINATION

*May they lay in peace where they fall*
*For they have fallen in a physical*
*Never shall they fall far from thy heart*
*I lust to join thee*
*Fire or water together we stay*
*finally you rest*
*Still sad I live*
*Until my restless destination*
*We will meet again*

I CONTINUE TO SURVIVE THE DANGERS OF THE BATTLEFIELD, BUT death haunts me, threatening to break my spirit, and traps me in my world. With devastating explosions of loss everywhere I turn, back to back, the people closest to me die. Kody, who is like a sister to me, Rel, who I would die for, and Slash, who I gang bang with. I give up dodging the bullet and mark myself for death.

*"If she's not strong enough to breathe once taken off the monitor, I'm sorry to say but we won't be able to save her."*

The words sound hollow in my ears: my friend Dee is lying in a hospital about to die. I am immobilized by grief. JP, her brother, is on the verge of committing suicide.

Dee suffers brain damage after a severe asthma attack. She is unconscious and breathing through a respirator. I feel helpless in the fight to save Dee, and even more helpless that JP is losing his mind. His face shows no emotion and his spirit seems to have moseyed away from his body.

Desperation sets in. I don't know how to console him, but know he needs to be.

It's hard to see her filled with tubes. She can't move, talk, or blink. She reminds me of my mom in Maryland, unconscious, tongue hanging out of her mouth.

The doctor comes in and informs us that they're taking Dee off the respirator in an hour.

"What if she can't breathe on her own?" I rebut.

Dr. Radison rubs a hand over his mustache and expels a deep breath.

I don't understand what he means but know that if Dee doesn't wake up soon, they're pulling the plug. Meanwhile, JP is yelling down the doctor's throat. "You ain't taken her off shit, motha-fucka! Don't come back in here!"

It reminds me of a baseball player yelling and kicking dirt on an umpire, only this is no game. I know he's going to flip out if Dee doesn't make it. For the entire hour we have with her before they come back, I whisper in her ear over and over, "Dee wake up . . . they gon' to take you off the machine. It ain't your time; please wake up!" My pleas go unanswered as she lies there with tubes in her nose, arms, and mouth. *You don't belong here.* I put my hand over her arm to feel connected to her. I wonder if she can hear me, but she is just unable to respond. JP's in deep distress and seems far gone as he stares into space.

"J, she's gonna make it, trust me."

Without looking at me, he responds, "Really," in a childlike tone. His eyes are vacant, spiritless. He knows she isn't going to pull through and it's beginning to sink in. There's no mistaking that his frustrations are etched into the veins bulging from his neck. He glares at me furiously. I break eye contact because it leaves me feeling uncomfortable. "Why won't she talk to me?" JP asks. Assuming this is a rhetorical question, I choose not to answer because truth is, I don't have a clue. For a moment he looks baffled, and then he goes to pieces with tears jumping out of his face. I used to hear that if you speak to a person who's in a coma, they can actually hear you. In this case we will never know since the doctor soon reappears. Dee is removed from life support.

JP had always been ambitious and goal-oriented. He loves playing basketball and dreams of playing in the NBA. Since Dee's death, however, he's been a zombie, lifeless, and unmotivated.

They say when shit starts tumbling downhill it snowballs, because three months after Dee passes away, I'm at another grave site. Willie G is on my football team. He's a senior and I'm a sophomore. He treats me like a li'l brother.

In October 1996, I receive a phone call from Emilio. "Yo, Blood, Wil got . . . man yo, they . . . they . . . shot him in the fuckin' head. They said he was on the pay phone in 108, projects." I drop the phone, while tears start to flow. "Who da fuck cou—" I can't finish my thoughts before picking up the phone. "Who did it? You know where they from?" He doesn't have any solid information. I immediately hang up the phone and run to 108. Willie was pronounced dead on the scene. He had been shot once in the head.

In tribute to Willie, I wear his jersey over my shoulder before every coin toss for the next two seasons. Before every game, my teammates hold a moment of silence, and pray for Willie's family.

# SILENT CRIES

*Outside of a house*
*A house I once called love*
*Loving every chance I get closer to death*
*Surface not yet seen*
*If one was to ask me what is life*
*No reply would be my answer*
*My low is the dead's hell*
*Most comfortable with the bed I made*
*My only hope is that the lord allows me to lay in it*

I HAVE ATTENDED TOO MANY FUNERALS; THOUGHTS OF SUICIDE began to creep into my head. They say that once you hit rock bottom there's nowhere to go but up. In my case, up is not an option. Too much loss, overwhelming pain, and unbearable suffering have brought me down and I'm ready to go deeper—into the grave. I can't live in this life, in this world. So, in order for me to live, first I must die. It's time to go.

It is a cold January night and I am hanging out on the porch listening to Meggette's record of life's story. I am stunned as he presents his childhood as an almost uninterrupted scene. Mine is a fogged-out setting where the most hurtful memories are furthest away.

My earliest memory of Meggette is when we realized we had something in common, two rare occasions when we speak about the unspeakable. We pour our problems on each other to receive a cushion for hits we are taking. The volume gets turned up when the conversation of suicide is mentioned for the first time.

"Yo Dae, I'm tired of being poor, I mean I can't get a fucking break. I'm tired of mothafuckas dying. I'm sick of eating that same shit every night, and I'm sick of biting, clawing, and scratching just to get a little something."

"I'm tired too, ain't shit we can do about it. You know something Blood, that's why I hate rich mothafuckas. Dem fools don't have shit to worry about. They biggest problems be shit like what outfit I'm a wear tonight, or the damn waitress didn't situate my fucking fork properly next to the spoon."

"Dae, you ever think about what if we weren't here anymore?" he asks.

With no regards to the seriousness of this question I say, "Fuck you talkin' 'bout nigga?"

"Nah, I mean do you ever think about like . . . I'm saying though like we always talk about stopping this pain right?" I follow with a quick nod. "So what if there's a way we could control it and end it altogether?" Still in my own zone, I can't make the connection to Meggette's puzzle.

Eventually time will allow us to reconnect on the topic. We are hanging out in Colgate Park. Both of us are drinking 40s. Five or six months have elapsed since our last conversation about death. But as we begin to talk, the topic turns to suicide. "Yo, if you just took out a whole precinct, police got you cornered off but you have one hostage, a cop, what would you do?"

My response was an easy one which I believe led to Meggette feeling I might be sympathetic. "I'd blow the cop away and then myself. If they gon' take me, it'll be in a body bag."

As the night closes in, we deepen our conversation.

Meggette seems bothered by something. Although I don't ask him what's on his mind, he clearly wants to tell me something.

"Yo, you ever thought about killing yourself?" Only this time, unlike before, he's not asking hypothetically. There's slight uncomfortable silence for the next few seconds as I try to figure out where he's coming from.

"A few times, but I don't think I could go through with it," I say. Looking at Meggette, I can tell this conversation is leading down the wrong path. He starts tossing out different examples of suicide: burning himself to death, death by a bullet, drowning, getting hit by car, or cutting his throat. I begin to feel sorry for him. It catches me by surprise because I see him in a different light.

"Yo B, if you thinking about killing ya'self, then I'm a do it too."

"Stop fuckin around Dae, I'm dead-up, I ain't playing," he says.

As we make our way down Day Street, I watch him from the corner of my eyes as he repeatedly says, "We gon' do it?"

Later that evening, we unwind at Meggette's house. He's on the couch sound asleep, as thoughts start to rush at me. Meggette's questions grow on me, "We gon' do it," as it starts to look like a possible escape. He's more willing to take this route than I am, but I feed off his energy and his misery.

Just the thought of suicide is breathtaking. It makes me feel superior.

Misery and lost love have landed me in a place I don't want to be in. Numerous deaths over the years have taken their toll on me. I go to sleep at night not wanting to wake up the next morning. Meggette's question has opened up a whole new possibility to me. I used to intensely feel the power of life or death. Now I have turned it on myself.

My homees are wounded soldiers in a battle that can't be won.

The crazy thing is most of us don't realize this until we get life behind bars, dead, or crippled. We put our lives on the line every day for streets and 'hoods we don't own.

We are trained to keep our society a secret, never snitch, and protect your brother. Codes and conducts taught from an early age are embedded in us. We are stuck between life and death, and feel comfortable only when angry, sad, and miserable.

It is my senior year in high school and Meggette is going through a crisis at home as I'm trying to get a grip on my own life. Suicide isn't just overdosing, hanging, or shooting oneself. To voluntarily walk the streets knowing that it can be your last day just because of a color you wear can be suicide. Between lack of money, family support, direction, purpose, and love, Meggette and I decide to love each other in the most absolute form, dying together.


Meggette and I meet in an abandoned building on Day Street. When we arrive we greet each other as we always do, with a firm brotherly hug and clenched fist. The plan is simple: we will play Russian roulette. What's distinctive about this game is the game's winner is also the game's loser. Meg brings a book bag full of Steel Reserves while holding E&J in his hand to get us there mentally. We drink and pump each other up to a point where there's no turning back. We stare at one another with looks that pose the question: "Do you really want to go through with this?" The whole time we are drinking and looking at each other, we never say a word. It's so quiet, we can hear each other breathing. We want to test our fate. We both are tearing up and hugging each other. We turn our cell phones off, write personal letters to our families and stick them on the walls. These letters are to be read if we don't make it out. Since two went in with a plan, either two are coming out alive or two are going to be dead. In our letters, we explain our actions, and that we are sorry for what's taking place. We sit down at a broken table, and give each other a moment-of-truth look. There're no smiles, blinks, grins, or looking away. It's time to challenge fate. Years and years of self-hate and violence on top of neglect and abuse have brought us to this moment. We debate on who will go first, and how will we decide? We ponder for a few minutes before Meggette says, "Fuck it, I'll go first." I reply, "Hell no Blood, I'm going first. You ain't leaving me first." We both want to prove to the other who loves who more.

We agree to engage in a tap-out match to decide who will test their fate first. Tap matches are something we do to resolve minor or major disputes about various situations we can't come to a mutual understanding on. We will fight it out until one of us hits the ground or surrenders. This match will be decided by whoever falls to the ground first. We take a few more drinks before we tangle up.

We begin tussling and swinging each other around hoping for a slam. There's no going easy because we take this matter very seriously. We wrestle for two minutes but it feels longer. We are sweating and grunting. What ends the fight is a body slam that lands Meggette to the ground with the sign of defeat all over his face.

The .38 is placed on the table all shined up, while we continue guzzling liquor. Five bullets are removed except the special one, the death bullet. We keep constant eye contact, and start.

As I approach Meg with the piece in my hand, he closes his eyes while biting his bottom lip. I take one spin of the barrel before clicking the gun closed. CLICK. The sound alone humbles Meg. He's trembling a bit sitting in the chair. I slowly approach him with the gun pointed at his head. One would have thought it was 10 below by the way I am shaking. Nevertheless, inch by inch I squeeze the trigger until we both hear the unforgettable sound:

CLICK! "Was that close or what Blood?" Meg stands up and says "Fuck!" He sounds disappointed the attempt failed. We embrace each other. We take a few more drinks before switching positions. What's fucked up about this situation is that if the gun goes off this time, Meg has to turn it on himself. Keeping in mind our purpose, if one goes we both go. Once we both get ready for the next round, I think, *Do I really want to go through with this?* The room is floating and I don't have a care in the world. I feel cocky, almost wishing the world could see me now. With the fact that Meg just went, I can't punk out, I have no choice but to take my turn. The barrel is spun once more and the trigger squeezed. What's more nerve-racking than anything is I can hear the trigger slowly approaching launch point. *Is this the way I want to go out?* The war is taking place right in my head. I am officiating. The winner of this battle is the loser in life's war. It takes forever for the trigger to reach its launch point. I picture my brains splattered all over the floor. My heart pounds like a set of bass drums. The idea of being dead and gone is gut-wrenching. As the seconds close in on the trigger being pulled, I take one last look in Meggette's eyes and say, "Do it mothafucka!" CLICK! is the next sound. I shout again, "Do it again! Again!" Each time getting louder and louder, "Now! Now! Now!" CLICK! My heart beats crazily and I feel a sharp pain in my chest. I'm sweating profusely and my pants are wet. We stayed true to our word, played our "game" and realize we are meant to be here. Why had we chosen to test our fate? It's only the excitement of being on the verge of death that reminds me of living. Minutes after the failed attempt we sit at opposite ends of the room staring at each other.

*What the hell just happened? Where do we go from here?*

We look into each other's eyes. We have long, deep, and meaningful conversations without moving our lips.

We loll around for hours afterward.

• • •

This is not the first time I try to commit suicide; it's just the most traumatic one.

After my homee Speedy was killed on his bike, I became suicidal on my bike. He was killed on his bike riding drunk. I thought many of times before he died of going out like he did. Months after his death, I get hit on my bike on the same block Speedy died on. Lying on the ground in pain and dizziness, Speedy's brother Rasheed pulls up in a cab. He's the first person I see once I can open my eyes. He helps me up, dusts me off, and says something to me that I will never forget.

*"Don't end up like my brother Dae."*

# PLAN B

*Where is the inventor of I*
*Product of his is most beautiful*
*Eyes of my mother tell me so*
*An owner every item deserves*
*I just knew my brother's creator would love me*
*Far lost then a beginning of I*
*For the doors of his home were open*
*But the doors to heart will forever be closed*
*Product I am not to be sold in the Ghetto*
*I am now a product of the Ghetto*
*Bang up scratch and scar*
*Depositable bin here I come!!!*
*Future of my rest will be an invention grave site*
*Feature of my to be seen by and inventor other then mine*
*For I possess the feature of life*
*Through life I shall live*
*Look! Look! I am a real boy now*

SOME MYSTERIES JUST NEVER DIE. INSTEAD, THEY HAUNT YOU throughout your life, possessing the power to torture your mind and batter your soul. For me, my absent father is the unsolvable puzzle. In stumbling through my life, I believe in the possibility of someday turning the corner that leads to him. That once I find him, I'll somehow find myself.

I met Coach Hoop during my sophomore year in high school. He was the quarterback coach, therefore we were bonded together. Coach Hoop's son, Jason, was also on the team playing wide receiver/safety. A few times, I contemplated quitting the team, but Coach Hoop not only fought to keep me, he motivated me to be the best quarterback to ever play at Orange High School. I didn't think I would have so much pressure on me, even though I was the starting quarterback. I often felt overwhelmed. I didn't get along with the coaching staff, except for Coach Hoop. He was the only one who was patient with me and pushed me to be great. I spent a lot of time at his house learning about the game of football. In addition, I learned a lot about how to conduct myself as a man on and off the field. Through his example, I learned what makes a good family man, putting your children's needs before your own. However, it would take some time for me to apply these lessons to my life.

Besides football, one of the many things we spoke about was a topic that I was uncomfortable discussing, my father. Coach tried to get me to talk about him but I had nothing to say, except that I wished Coach was my father. He also asked about my stepfather, Norman, who I lived with for all four years of high school and on and off before that when we were living in New Jersey.

Imagine living with a person in whose presence you feel unimportant. My stepfather always looks at me scornfully, and turns up his nose as if a skunk has just entered his front door. He walks around with a "leave me alone" look on his face. He arches his shoulders and projects his voice as if he and he alone is the answer to all matters. You would think due to his vows to my mother, he'd love me unconditionally. I ask why, where, and when did he decide to cripple me without even touching me?

He always criticizes me. He is very insecure. My personality threatens his well-established, inflated ego. The negative seeds he planted in my head took root, grew, and eventually live in me, his Blood now becoming mine. Years of neglect, mental abuse, and resentment dwell in me. His cruelty pumps through my Blood. My presence is a constant source of irritation to him, and breaking down the walls of separation seems impossible. By my senior year of high school he and my mother were still living together. It's one thing to feel rejected when we moved from place to place, but to feel discarded in my own home is another.

Norman failed in all aspects of fatherhood. There was so much he withheld from us: love, hugs, talks, bonding times, and life lessons that only a pops could teach. I remember at a young age, I'd ask questions:

"Where do babies come from?"

"What is this?" pointing to my penis.

"What are these?" pointing to a woman's breasts.

He never answered me.


In four years, Coach Hoop taught me more than my stepfather did in my entire life. I have a huge amount of respect for him. He is an extremely intelligent man with a lot of charisma that translates into a powerful presence. When Coach speaks, all eyes and ears are open. I admire his relationship with his son. They have father-and-son outings, and Coach always teaches Jason lessons about life. Important lessons like how to be a man, how to think like a man, how to act like a man, and how to live as a man.

At Coach Hoop's house, I see him hug Jason and tell him he loves him. Coach doesn't know it, but the sight of this kills me. *Where is my father? Why couldn't he hug me and tell me he loved me?* When Coach would hug me, I would feel weird inside because I didn't know what it was like to have male affection. It made me feel really uncomfortable. I wonder if he sensed this.

During my junior year in high school, my mom stumbled upon one of my family members from my father's side of the family. Through that connection, she was able to get the phone number to my half-sister, Sara, who lives in Newark with my father. I'm hesitant to call, but Mom encourages me. After all these years of thinking about him, I finally have the opportunity to meet him. *What will I say? What will he think of me?* I work up enough courage to dial his number. A strong, deep, raspy voice answers the phone as I struggle to get the words out.

"Is Art there?"

"This is him, whose calling?"

"Dashaun. I got cha number from Aunt Greda."

"Hey, wassup boy? How ya been?"

We start talking like we've known each other for years. We go into conversation about various things about my life for the last fifteen years. Finally, he asks me to visit. I look forward to meeting the rest of my siblings. We talk for thirty minutes before hanging up. I think about his offer to go see him, contemplating whether I even want to go. *After all these years, I gotta go. I gotta put a face on all the long years of imagining.*

We would have our first chance to talk man-to-man. But there were fifteen years of abandonment and hostility festering. I see this as my chance to ask all of my unanswered questions.

A week later I drive to his house. The house is in bad condition. There's trash all around. There are three kids out front drawing on the sidewalk with color chalk. *Could these be Sara's kids, my nieces and nephews?* Can't say any of them look like me but I have a strong feeling that they are. I sit in the car a few minutes watching them play before heading to the door.

*What will he look like? Is he going to be anything like me? Will I be disappointed?*

With my head bowed, studying the grass as though it contains the answers to life's mysteries, I walk up to the door. My heart pounds. I've been so focused on my mission to meet my father that I didn't take time to reflect on the weight of the occasion. *I'm meeting my father for the first time.* I don't know whether to be elated or angry. I am both.

When I walk into the house, there waiting for me in the kitchen is my half-brother and sister, Saliq and Sara, and five of my nieces and nephews. One by one, Sara introduces me to my relatives. Three of them are Sara's and the other two are Saliq's. To my surprise, Saliq is a cop. *My brother is a cop?* As we begin to talk, my father finally emerges from a back room. He's six foot three and thin. He has a smooth and boyish face full of hair. He wears a tank top with khaki color pants, and has a Kangol on. We look too much alike. He might have ignored me for my entire life, but he could never deny that I was his son. Looking at my father is like viewing myself after a twenty-five-year digital age progression. We share many of the same features, smooth mocha complexion, chinky eyes, and perfect teeth. I can't say any of my drawings of him from childhood are accurate.

As he nears me, I get a twinge inside. I know a hug is coming. I don't want a hug from him. I don't even know him, this strange man that looks just like me. We embrace one another with a pat on the back. I notice he has rings on every finger. We keep eye contact as we are both feeling each other out. Art clears his throat before motioning for me to follow him to the back.

The room is crammed with junk everywhere. Socks here,

shoes there, trash on the bed, and a carpet that needs to be burned. The room smells of years and years of dust, dirt, and filth. There's a Black couch in his room that seems to have surrendered to the weight of the loads and loads of clothes, jackets, shirts, and anything else that would fit on it. Seconds later, two of his grandkids are in the doorway. Art demands, "Y'all get outta here, and go back to the living room." His tone changed to one I gather sent the message with no problem because they did exactly as they were told. He then motions for me to take a seat on the couch while lighting a cigar. I remain standing.

"You can throw that stuff in the corner over there," he says. "You look . . ." Father starts.

" . . . just like you," I respond, finishing his sentence. I sit next to him on the couch. I shiver. I have goose bumps from sitting so close to this man who's haunted me my whole life. He studies me, zooming in for a deeper look.

"Christ. I haven't seen you since you were born. You're a good-looking kid."

I clear my throat. I consider a dozen different openings and, in an instant, discard them all. I opt to cut to the chase.

"Good-looking *man*," I say, overemphasizing *man*. "You can drop that kid shit. Those days are over; you missed 'em, Pops." I used as much mockery as I could summon.

My words seem to hit him like a punch to the stomach. Pops grimaces, lowers his head, and shoves his hands in his pockets. His reaction answers my question: he's a loser.

"Fair enough," Pops says soberly. "I thought about you a lot, you know. Wondered how you were doing."

Pops takes out his handkerchief, blots his forehead, and then holds the cloth against his lips as though trying to hold in the words that want to spill out.

He wipes his mouth, and then puts the cloth against his forehead again, sopping up a fresh layer of sweat. He draws in a breath. I pause.

"I never meant to hurt you," he says.

"What kind of man would disown his child?"

Pops glares at me. "Why are you so upset?" The disturbing question lodges in my mind like a splinter.

I can't think of an adequate reply. I feel tears trying to seep through my eyes. I have too much pride to give him that pleasure, I fight them back. *I should have known better,* I thought. *What kind of response did I expect to hear? A tearful confession? A heartfelt apology?*

"You got a lot of balls to corner me like this," Pops says. As if I was accountable for my own upbringing.

"Do you know who I am, boy?"

I cross my arms feeling a bit awkward at his question.

"Let me tell you who I am," Pops says, squaring his shoulders. "I am your father, Dashaun. You may not agree with my decisions, but you have no right to judge me. I did what I did because . . . I had to."

*Liar, I hate you,* I think.

"I don't know what else I can say," Pops says. "The truth is, I'm glad to see you."

"Bullshit, you ain't gotta say that to make me feel better."

Pops winces, looks around as though worried who might over-hear us. "Do you have to curse so much?"

"What? You see me for the first time in fifteen years and all you can say is don't curse?"

"Forget it," Art says. "All right, then. Why are you here? What do you want from me, Dashaun?"

"You really wanna know?" I said.

"You want money, is that it? How much?"

*Is he serious!* I leap to my feet. I'm about to lose control, and have to catch myself. This isn't the way I wanted this conversation to go.

"Hell no, I don't want no money!"

"If it's not about money, then what is it?" Art spreads his arms. "Tell me, what is this all about?"

"Where the fuck you been?"

I sit down again, and count to ten in my head.

"I want to be a part of your family," I say softly. "I want to be like you and Saliq are. I want to be a part of the family too."

He looks at me. "You're serious."

Now he stands and puts his fists on his waist, pacing the room like I asked him a trick question.

He glances at me, eyebrows arched. "I have a life here, Dashaun. There are too many problems around here as it is."

"I'm your son. You haven't seen me for years, and you are telling me about your problems. What about mine? What about all the problems I had to deal with?"

Pops frowns, and lowers his head as if he's just been defeated.

"I'm not the sole decision-maker around here," Art says. "I need to talk to Irene." Referring to his wife.

"Come on, you're the man of the house," I challenge. "She ain't got nothing to do with us."

"It's not that easy."

"So you mean to tell me, you gotta ask her if your own flesh and blood be a part of your life."

The rest of our conversation went no better.

I stayed for an hour before flat-lining home. When I get back, I tell my mother how our meeting went. She seems pleased that I have finally reunited with my real father. For the first time she sits me down and tells me about him.

In my mother's room we have a heart-to-heart. She gives me the hidden truth about the real man my father was. I am shocked and angered to find out about their past. "Art was an evil man. He abused me."

I think, *You can't be serious.* But she's not joking.

How could she have allowed him to harm her like that? Their relationship was over before ever getting started. While pregnant with me, Mama met my younger brother's father. She blames her relationship full of abuse on being in love with my father. I plan on paying Art another visit.

Ten-thirty the following night, I toss on my gear and drive to his house with two of my relatives. I'm strapped and ready to tax his ass.

Boogie and Arnel accompany me. "Y'all stay down here until I'm done. I'm a handle this shit real quick."

Heading upstairs, the heavy aroma of weed fills the stairway. I take the steps two and three at a time. Inside, there's music and television playing simultaneously.

Entering the house, I walk down the hallway looking for him in his room first. I shove the door open to find it empty. I quickly glance into various rooms; they're empty. I head back toward the dining room where I hear laughter. I make my way down the hallway; there, Art sits with his wife, Irene, and one of their friends. They're playing cards, drinking, and getting high. Art gives me a nonchalant look while shuffling the cards.

"Hey son, what are you doing here?"

His condition doesn't allow him to recognize danger.

"Say what mothafucka!" I charge him with the force of Ray Lewis behind me.

As I wrestle him down to the ground, he repeatedly shouts, "What the hell is wrong with you? Stop fucking around!"

Once I am on top of him, I trash him. I take the strap out and begin beating him ferociously. Blood squirts everywhere, covering the walls.

Before I know it I am staring down the barrel of a 9mm. When Saliq whips out the heat, the noise of a round being chambered sends a paralyzing chill over me. I still have Art yoked up by the neck with one hand and the other hand now pulls out my gun and points it at Saliq. *Where the hell did he come from?* The fact that Saliq is a police officer doesn't cross my mind because all I see is a gun, and for that it doesn't matter who he is.

"Dashaun, drop the gun now!"

"Do you know this mothafucka used to beat my mother?"

He doesn't pay any attention to my comments. He repeats himself in a slower and more demanding voice.

"Put the gun down!" Still fully enraged, I continue to assault my father, calling Saliq's bluff. Before I know it, the weight of a man is on my back. It's Saliq.

"I got him!" Saliq yells.

Saliq's a few inches shorter than me, but a hundred pounds heavier. I try to shake him off, but it's useless. "Fuck you! Let me go."

He grasps me tighter, sucking the air out of me. His arms choke me. I grab his back arm, but he recovers fast. "Let me go!" I shout louder.

I can't get him off me. I can't run. *He gonna lock me up.*

In desperation to get away, I turn my gun on Saliq. Saliq's breath is hot on my neck; his arms strangle me. I reach over my shoulders and aim.

He flinches, but his arms tighten. "Get the fuck off me!" I demand again.

I stretch my hand beneath my underarm and fire.

The shot misses. He releases me, I stand. He draws his weapon again. "Put it down now! Don't make me do this! I'm not gonna ask you again, Dashaun, put the fucking gun down!"

My stance is ready, like a sharpshooter. My hands grip my gun tighter than they should, my adrenaline surges. I'm ready.

"Hold on, Dashaun. Let's talk." He tries to diffuse the situation.

Then Art's voice rises. "Get the fuck outta here!"

I give him a vicious stare. "Fuck you!" My voice is filled with hate and rage. This ain't over.

At this point, I let go of Art's shirt, which sends him crashing to the ground.

"You put yo' shit down nigga?" I challenge Saliq. At this point you can't tell me this isn't going to end in gunfire.

"Now you know I can't do that. Don't do this."

I thought about it for a second and realized Saliq wasn't going to shoot me, or was he?

"If I lower mine, you gon' lower yours?"

Inch by inch we both lower our guns. I don't blink. Art's on the floor groaning and moaning, covered in blood. Saliq bellows, "Dashaun just leave!"

I take off down the front stairs where Boogie and Arnel wait.


At home later, I jump in the shower to wash off my body, which is covered with my father's Blood. I sleep well that night.

That was the last time I saw my father. I walked away and never looked back. To this day, he has not bothered to come looking for me. In true form, he has never given me anything or done anything to improve my life. And at this point, I don't want anything from him. I've moved on and I have no expectations that he has any interest in me. But one thing is certain: I will never be like him. I found out who I was as a result of our meeting, and for the first time I realized I am not him; I'm better.

•  •  •

In the fall of 1999, I begin my senior year. I suppose every high school senior feels some anxiety, but I am gripped by fear because of what the year symbolizes—my expected entry into the real world.

My senior season marked a tradition and long-lasting legacy at Orange High School. I worked out all summer prior to the season, and knew this would be the year I broke out. I attended the Penn State football camp during the summer where I became well acquainted with Eli Manning of the New York Giants, who was there as well. I came back prepared for the season.

Our first game is against the number two team in the state, Delbarton. They had won consecutive state championships and expected us to be a walk in the park.

I am the leader of a complicated run-and-shoot offense that is designed to score lots of points. Heading to Bell Stadium after school, I wear my most intense face. I am completely focused on winning the game.

As the team readies for battle all dressed in our colors of lightning orange, I stand before the team and deliver an intense pep talk.

"Look, we practiced all week; no, we practiced all summer for this moment. All the talk is about them, but today is our day. We gon' play they kinda ball smash mouth."

This speech among all the previous ones held a different kind of weight. I see it in their eyes. They look at me like a village would their leader. When Head Coach Daniels approaches the team he is pleased to see that he has a group of pumped-up players. He delivers a short lethal message straight from Tom Landry's handbook. When we take the field for warmups, we are eye-to-eye with our adversaries, Delbarton.

The Spartans are dressed in shiny grassy green uniforms outlined in silver. Their running back Jermaine Pugh is nothing short of Barry Sanders and is the talk of the state. At five foot four, 180 pounds, he's sure to run circles around us.

Before kickoff, Coach Hoop ends his speech with his all-time favorite quote, "We got garbage to take out, and the house smells like shit."

Today is every bit of a historic day in Orange, New Jersey. The team responds to Coach's leadership by doubling our intensity with every play. For the next two and a half hours, Delbarton gets its first dose of, not only a Blood wit' an arm, but a Blood wit' brains.

At one point, Meggette lets loose a passionate wail, "If you scared, get a dawg!" My energy skyrockets.

At the end of the first quarter it's Orange 7, Delbarton 0. Through the Bloody battle we beat Delbarton 20–14. We put ourselves on the map as one of New Jersey's top programs. I threw one touchdown and ran in two. This game alone opens doors for me to receive scholarships to many universities.

My senior season success earns me a spot in New Jersey's East vs. West All-Star game. I'm named 1st team all-conference, 1st team all-county, and 1st team all-area. Ironically, I play wide receiver in the statewide game instead of my usual position as quarterback. I score two touchdowns and rack up two catches for 107 yards. I cherish playing high school football, because it's the only time I can recall being a part of something that was productive.

I spend the last few months before graduation in a deep fog. Time blurs. The graduation calendar reminds me that my being on my own is coming.

Saint and I discuss the direction of the set and what our roles should be. Ultimately, he decides to go into the army.

Before graduation, I have a conversation with Coach Hoop about what happens next. He challenges me about my future in the gang. His ultimate question resonates in my head. *Can I move on out of the gang life and be a man?*

Coach urges me to go to college and pursue a football career. My senior football season awarded me acceptance letters from Syracuse, Hofstra, Rutgers, and a few Division 1-AA schools. I ponder the thought that life may have something else in store for me, but the 'hood makes it cloudy to see clear. A few times I talk with the homees about me going to college. I get chuckles and insults.

"NIGGA you ain't going to college, college is fo' White motha-fuckas B." But a lot of what Coach Hoop said to me makes a lot of sense.

Is there life after the gang?

# PEOPLE PLACES AND THINGS

*Eyes in a sky*
*An unlawful truth has been born*
*For land I walk is all that eyes have seen*
*Flesh of mine has never left my hell*
*A hell where all souls look the same*
*Things I know are from another devil's past*
*A place of free is where I want to be*
*Confused as I was at birth*
*Born again I rise*

In 2000 I enroll at Delaware State University. After ten years of gang life, and burying homees, I can't take it no more. With all the attention I received from college scouts after my senior season in high school, college looked like a great way to start over.

Six months earlier, Saint leaves for the army in Louisiana. Before he leaves we make a pact that after taking care of business in our newfound obligations, we'd return to apply our knowledge and skills to benefit the set. I see college as my stepping-stone to the NFL, which will enable me to secure a comfortable lifestyle for my family.

Being new and feeling awkward in an unfamiliar environment is old news for me. It's the story of my life. So, when the semester starts and I arrive on campus, it's the same ol' same ol' I've been experiencing my whole life. I feel like an outsider.

The students here are not like the people from Newark. They're bright-eyed, excited, and very much into their studies. The professors are courteous, humble, and concerned for the progress of their students.

Always on alert, one of my many tasks here is spotting my enemies. Here, they wear blue flags, orange flags, purple flags, and red flags as a form of fashion.

Immediately, I think there are Crips and Bloods here. The first guy I approach wearing a red bandanna is clueless.

"Wess brackin' Blood? You Loc'n?"

"Am I what?" he says while arching his eyebrow with confusion stamped all over his face.

"Kllaaattt killah," I shout while throwing up a P with my left hand, and CK with my right. Sizing him up, reading him for any signs that indicate enemy, I remove my razor from my mouth.

"Oh n-na-na-na-nooo, I ain't down wit no gangs or nothing."

"Say what! Let me get that boo-boo from you Blood." I point to the garbage tied around his head. Without hesitation he hands it over to me.

Football is the reason I came here. Excited about reporting for summer camp, I'm upset to find out that I won't be able to participate my first season. I want to play now, but sitting out a year has its advantages.

I wait patiently for my turn, and pay my dues all summer. I watch my teammates Darnerien McCants of the Philadelphia Eagles score eighteen collegiate touchdowns; Albert Horsey run routes around defensive backs; and Jamal Jackson of the Philadelphia Eagles pancake block every defensive lineman in the conference.

The new year, 2001, is finally here and I am ready to play. I work myself into the starting wide receiver's position. I have a decent season racking up five touchdowns for 550 yards and thirty-three catches.

Although my eyes are set on the NFL, it's difficult to abandon gang banging.

While maintaining my leadership position at school, months elapse without me putting work in for the set. My hunger for hunting Crips decreases, although I still hate Crips. My ghetto armor begins to soften.

The irony is that for the first time in my life, I am relaxed. Bangin' isn't even a factor. People get along here. I'm beginning to see what else the world has to offer besides gang bangin', but only to myself will I admit it. What good has come out of banging for me? We drop some of them, and they drop some of us. Who is actually winning? I am growing tired of the shootouts, drugs, and being responsible for the minds of murderers. Having to face your homee's moms after he's been murdered is beyond explainable. Assuming that you've never been through this, I won't take you down that path; not yet.

Coming to college was the hardest thing for me to do.

Playing football clears my mind of knowing all the things that are going on back home with drugs, deaths, and gang wars. And yet, I am still in charge of my entire set along with Saint. I'm the shot-caller. With all these distractions, it becomes impossible to focus on school. Being pulled in so many directions combined with being in a new place, away from my family, causes a lot of stress. Living this double life I have too much on my shoulders. Both worlds demand my attention.

Case in point, at 2:37 A.M. on a Wednesday my cell phone rings, opening my eyes, waking me up from a deep sleep. I see eight missed calls. I'm needed. I clear my throat before answering.

"Sooo Woop, yo, we caught dis Brab."

I ask him to repeat himself.

"Yeah . . . yeah . . . wass up wit' dat funk now? You gon' die tonight Crab mothafucka. Machete? Machete? Machete can you hear me? We got one. Mothafucka say he ain't crippin', but he got on a blue and gray flag. Shut the fuck up Crab!" I hear muffling and tussling in the background.

I look at my phone and realize it's my lieutenant E with Dough. Now sitting up in my bed, I'm alert.

"Yo . . . yo . . . yo . . . what the funk going on!"

"Blood, we caught a Brab slippin' out Dodd Town, he trying to deny his 'hood, but I know dis mothafucka Crip. Can I ruff sex 'em?"

"I ain't a Crip; I swear to God, I'm telling you," the Crip pleads. Still digesting, I realize someone is about to die. My brain tells me to give the go-ahead, but my heart tells me otherwise.

"Machete, you there Blood? Wassup! Fuck this mothafucka; he probably killed some homees befo'." I hear Dough in the background ordering the Crip not to move. E has the gun to the Crip while we speak on the phone. I want to say yes, I want to eliminate another Crip. I wonder during the five-minute conversation what's going through the mind of this Crip as he waits for his life to be determined from the other end of a cell phone. I sense the excitement in E's voice as he repeats.

"Come on Blood, fuck dis Crab, I got dis, come on Blood."

My mind flashes back to a night when Crips caught me slipping on Norfolk Street leaving New Hope Village. Leaving Drip's apartment dressed down in my uniform, flag around my head, I head home. It's somewhere around 10:00 P.M. as I cross the street. Putting my key into the door, a van pulls up on me with straps aiming. I have no gun. Once the owners of the vehicle show their faces, I'm welcomed by four masked gunmen all with blue flags covering their face.

"One-eleven, slob ass snoop!"

I was certain I was dead on sight. One of the Crips waves a blue bandanna out of the window in an up-and-down motion signaling, We caught yo' ass slippin'.

I want to make a run for it, but they're too close.

"Look at cho punk ass now, all scared and shit. What chu bangin' slob?"

"P-funk." I don't respond with hostility or aggression. Just a voice filled with defeat. I begin thinking about the coffin I'll be in.

"Die mothafuckin' RU, Clllaaattt, dat's right Snoop, N'hood, two and a thumb, killing all Floods. Cuz ain't ready to die." The passenger snatches my flag off my head. *Mothafucka! They poppin' shit, then they gon' smoke me, damn!* But then they do something I didn't expect. They close the van door, throw my flag out the window in flames, and peel off. This is a form of gang bangin' disrespect. *On B'z I'm a kill dem mothafuckas!*

In bangin' culture, it's insulting to do something like this. It was done to humiliate me, and they got their point across. Any banger who has ever been through this, knows that this is the biggest form of disrespect. I thought about it the entire night when I got home and many thereafter. They laughed at and patronized me. After that episode, I had an even more indescribable hate for Crips. Needless to say, I cured my humiliation with revenge.

I seldom thought about that moment again until I received the phone call from Dough and E with the P.O.B., prisoner of Blood. Out late, caught slippin' just like I once was. Slippin' is the biggest penalty for gang bangin'. While you think you pulling over to get a burger, another fool is on his job. Rule number one of bangin': fuck the rest; you got to be on the clock 24/7 because when you punch out, an enemy just clocked in.

The decision to kill the Crip is easy, but the memory of receiving a pass myself gives me empathy for the fool.

"Let 'em go E."

"What Blood?" Obviously catching the homee by surprise.

"Let 'em live."

"Stop playin' Blood, you berious. Did you hear what I said, I got one?"

"Yo fuck dat fool, let 'em pass."

"Yo big homee, this mothafucka lying, str8 loccin, I'm telling you."

"He probably is, but fuck 'em, next time."

"Aiigghhtt! Aiighhtt! You got dat Blood, but I'm telling you, you should let me smoke 'em."

In the background I could hear them taunting the Crip. "You lucky mothafucka."


I met Raheem the most obvious way one B-Dawg discovers another, by his dress code. We pass each other our freshman year when his logo caught my attention. He, a proud sponsor of his 'hood, was wearing a Black T-shirt with gigantic red letters G.K.B., Gangster Killer Bloods, emblazoned across the chest, and a Kansas City Chiefs hat.

I step to Blood to see what dat B like.

"What it RU, what dat FUNK like?" At the same time we do the gangsta shake. With his stomping grounds being New York and mine Jersey, there was a bit of a mix-up in our greeting ritual; nonetheless, we made do. We interlocked our hand and fingers in various ways to signify we were forever connected.

He shot back in a low voice, "Raheem from G.K.B." I'm sure he could tell I was a relative of his, from the burgundy laces that blessed my fresh Black Chucks, and my burgundy Dickies shirt.

My vibe is so powerful that sometimes I hypnotize people by merely being in their presence. The keys to my strength are my devotion and dedication. The word Blood is so powerful that it is heard from coast to coast, L.A. to N.J. Even in Asia. And now I'm representing on a college campus where most parents send their kids thinking it will be safe.

The word Blood has such an infinite reach, that to call someone Blood in Canada, they'd embrace you and throw it up. I'm connected to brothers all over this country and even internationally. We see each other dressed down, we don't speak but we visually connect. The unspoken is often more effective than what is said.

One day while leaving my dorm, I G-stroll across the yard mumbling some lyrics by the Relatives. Already feeling superior to the general pop, I amp up my swagger. I'm rockin' a pair of Black sweat pants, a burgundy T-shirt, burgundy New Balance on my feet, and my affiliation on my shoulder exposed for the general public to feel my presence. One would think I was screamin' out loud, but I'm not. My colors are too loud? I take full advantage of the stares I'm getting from onlookers jocking me. With my box braids only one day old, and the sun gleaming off my tight-ass parts. In contrast to the general population, I seem an exotic import.

Almost at my destination, I am stopped by Raheem, who interrupts my G-stroll. After removing his red N.Y. Yankees cap and wiping his forehead with his bandanna, I greet the brother as he begins giving me the details about who, what, where, when, and why.

"Yo," still trying to retrieve his second wind, "I got into a beef earlier today, and I wanna go check da nigga."

Once he reveals all the pertinent particulars, my reaction reveals what my heart feels—revenge.

Without needing much explanation I jump at the offer. "Where home bwoy at Blood?" I exhort.

His passive posture only confirms to me that he is either an advocate of Martin Luther King or just a plain old pussy. I can tell Blood ain't used to putting in work because he's too hesitant. Nonetheless, he is Blood. We flat-line to Camron's class. I'm ready to step to him when Raheem snorts in contempt. "Machete, I got this."

In a blasé voice I shoot back, "Whatever man."

As these two begin discussing their differences, I can't help but look at the homee in a dimmer light. I stand to the side in disgust watching these two bicker like kids over a PlayStation game.

*"Enough is enough. I don't get down like this,"* I interrupt, clenching my teeth in a growling whisper. "Yo Blood, I'm a bout to flat."

As a result, to the untrained eye, they patch shit up. However, to a student of the streets, it just means, "Right now ain't the time nor place, but I'll catch yo ass later." Or at least for me it does.

My only union with Raheem is our red flags, which in most cases can unite two complete strangers. Except something bugs me about his swagger, his wearing a red flag confuses my perception of him, and after his confrontation with Camron I have even less respect for him.

By the end of my first two semesters, the word spreads like wildfire that I am a Blood. Anyone who knows anything about gangs can tell by the way I dress and speak. Red shoelaces, red Chucks, red beads in my hair, red flags, red everything . . . red red red! On a campus that never met anyone like me, my affiliation has a triple effect: it scares the hell out of them, attracts others wh are mesmerized by the Hollywood-style idea of gangs, and finally, gives me unwanted notoriety.

Back on the field, the summer is coming up to my junior year, and this is to be my breakout season. I train all summer, day and night, improve my route running, and become a better student of the game. Things are going well for me and I'm confident that my dreams of playing professional football will become reality.

# UPS AND DOWNS

*Are my cries allowed to die?*
*Joy I know took on pain's hand in marriage*
*A river from my face reflects my truth*
*Love they will not of what they don't know*
*Dream a dream on the tip of a mountain*
*Who cared that I conquer the top*
*I have tasted a greater joy*
*For I have also fallen*
*Now your smiles seem real*

DURING MY JUNIOR YEAR EVENTS IN MY LIFE START TO SNOW-
ball. As the series of events intensifies, time elongates. Days turn
to months and months to years.

It's December 9, 2002, and I'm expelled from Delaware State
for possession of a .380 handgun and ammunition on school
grounds. The expulsion destroys my football career, when I am
one step away from the NFL, shattering my world. It all starts
because of a campus beef between the football players and the fraternity Phi Beta Sigma.

I'm not that close to my teammates off the field. The Sigmas
are working up courage for a retaliation attempt on the football

players after a fight took place earlier in the day. On the night of December 8, while waiting to go the store, I'm passed by approximately twenty Sigmas. Some I know and some I don't. I notice one individual staring at me the entire time he passes by.

When he walks by, I challenge, "Wess hanniin Blood?"

He doesn't respond, but gives me a look like he wants some funk. I reach for my strap before catching myself. *I can't shoot him, too many witnesses*.

Later that night, back in my room, I get a knock at my door. When I answer, two school officers are standing there with a warrant to search my room for a gun. The entire time they search my room, I see my future. My football career is over before it starts. All my hard work is for nothing. When they retrieve the gun they cuff me and take me out. At the station, they question me about the gun, and ask if it's been used in a crime.

I'm eventually released later that night. I sleep at a motel and wait for my hearing trial.

I receive the dreaded letter the following morning. I am expelled. Immediately anxiety surges within me, and my life soon begins its spiraling descent.

My mom makes her way down the turnpike to Delaware. When she gets to my motel room, she embraces me with a firm and supportive hug. She comforts me like a mother should. But I don't want comfort, I need my future back. After an hour of containing my built-up anger, I storm out of the room, ending up at Silver Lake Park. It's past midnight and two friends of mine come looking for me.

"Dashaun I know you out here, come out!" Joel shouts.

I run away from the voices. I don't want to speak to anyone. I'm cold and tired. I feel completely hopeless.

My mom is back at the room crying because she doesn't know where I am. After running away from friends, I find myself running alongside Route 13. The temperature is in the teens, yet my anger boils hotter with each step I take. I know everything's lost and I want to escape it all. Completely distraught, I want to cause as much pain as possible to myself as punishment for my failures.

I picture the scene over and over in my head before attempting it, sirens blazing down Route 13 with traffic backed up a mile long, shattered bones, Blood on the ground. This fantasy begins to satisfy my desire to hurt myself.

I can't go any further, I'm exhausted and freezing. I stagger before catching myself. For a moment, I can't understand how I got here. As the oncoming traffic whizzes by at 65 mph, I go one-on-one with a pickup truck. I time it perfectly. I step in front of the truck, leaving the driver little time to avoid hitting me. My eyes haven't adjusted to the darkness so the high beams of the oncoming truck blind me from seeing the driver. Standing in front of the truck, I close my eyes. *Kill me you bastard*. In this moment, destiny steps in and takes over. It's not my time, no matter how bad I want it. The driver manages to avoid hitting me as he slams on the brakes. Swerving into the intersection, he rear-ends another turning vehicle. After the close twist of fate, I run into the park and find a bench to lie down on. Stretched out, I stare at the stars for hours. When I finally wake up I walk back to the hotel to face my mother.

# BLESSINGS IN
# THE MIDST OF THE FIRE

*There lies a tree*
*Dead leaves grow from its limbs*
*Lost souls piss on her*
*Others pour liquor on her*
*For the unforgotten souls*
*It was only when the moon and the sun rose at once*
*When I rose from the tree roots and broke through the dirt*
*I rise*
*Given the chance to create life from death*
*I rose*
*Standing tall as a tree should*
*All I have to show for my hell*
*Is my rose*

WHAT IS LOVE? BANGIN' AND BLIND LOYALTY TO MY HOMEES?
I'm convinced it's everything I'm committed to die for. But when
I open my heart and let "The One" walk in, she opens my eyes to
the real meaning of love—my future, my legacy, exposing me to
my own humanity, and everything I'm ready to live for.

By mid-February, I've lost fifteen pounds. I have gone two weeks without eating more than a piece of bread and some chips, and during this time I have become so thin I look like a raisin. I look terrible; my brown eyes are red-rimmed and bloodshot. My smooth, tan complexion looks rough and discolored.

I meet Nicole in a class we have together in 2001. She shares the same major, sports management, so we see a lot of each other. We are partners in class. Nicole is unique, unlike most of the campus girls. During our projects, she ends up doing more of my work than I do. She stays up with me until one and two in the morning helping me finish. I take a liking to the newfound treatment because I'm not used to people sincerely caring for me, except the gangsta love I receive from my homees. After all, this is different; Nicole is a positive and encouraging person who befriends me in my time of need.

I never met anyone so highly motivated, and full of life like Nicole. She goes to bat for me like her own brother. Since I can't live on campus anymore, Nicole takes me in. Most nights, she stays up trying to comfort me. I hibernate in Nicole's house every day, feeling worthless.

I have gone from being a future NFL draft pick to a suicidal, depressed maniac. Nicole tries to get me to come out of the house for air, but the darkness inside comforts me. She wants me to continue working out to help keep my mind off my situation, but I can't seem to find the energy to be strong during this crisis.

Finally, on February 22, I agree to go with Nicole to one of her frat brother's houses for a Mike Tyson fight party.

Once there, I find a spot in the corner and remain there most of the night. During the fight, Nicole introduces me to her line sister, Neina. Nicole and Neina are members of the Delta Sigma Theta sorority. There is something about her eager, large, inquiring Bambi-like eyes and feminine laugh that is both adorable and challenging. She has straight, jet-Black hair combed back in a ponytail. She also has the most voluptuous breasts I have ever seen. She sports a pair of blue jeans decorated by a full body of Delta accessories.

Midway through the night, Neina offers me a drink that I decline. I take this as her gesture of trying to break the ice. However, what Neina does is offer me the opportunity to meet my soul mate. The following day, talking to Nicole, I inquire about Neina. Nicole soon arranges a night for a few of her friends to go to TGIF. There, Neina and I speak more. She is really standoffish. I can't decipher her intentions. With Neina unaware of my situation, I'm reluctant to tell her about my expulsion and the reasons behind it. I hope she doesn't know already. She doesn't strike me as a city girl, let alone a girl that had any knowledge of the streets. Eventually, I muster enough courage to tell her about my troubles. She is immediately supportive and encouraging. She doesn't seem to be intimidated by me. This is the moment for her to take off. She stays. Without sugarcoating anything I explain my involvement with the Bloods.

We start seeing more and more of each other. Until this point, I have never felt comfortable explaining details about my past, but she puts me at ease and never passes judgment. She calls me throughout the day, giving me the feeling that everything is going to be okay. I'm falling for her—it is the first time I've felt this way; and as I express my feelings to her I gain a clearer understanding of who I am as a man.

In the intimacy of our space, the moment came when we finally shared our love and sealed our bond. Neina slowly takes off her clothes. Her body is erotic. She wraps her arms around me and presses herself against me. As she puts her lips to my ears she whispers, "That's enough foreplay."

Now, lying in the bed, she's ready for me. She squeezes her hips and thighs tightly together and relaxes them, and squeezes again, getting me more and more excited. She shifts her body slightly so that each sensation is different for me. She gives me a gift I had never imagined, stimulating me to an ecstatic pitch of excitement. She's the one.

Neina eventually gives birth to my firstborn daughter, Da-Shana Sani Morris. My baby girl is the turning point in my life. In her, I see myself, my value. She inspires my evolution as a man.

# GUARDIAN ANGELS

*In me to believe*
*One other than I*
*The question to be is why*
*For I've seen the darkest of my skies*
*A fear unthought of to be life*
*Foreign is the world, alone to roam*
*Clouded was a mind never to know*
*Unseen was an angel for only love to see*
*Blind were thee eyes only to see hate against I*
*For they see a light of worth*
*A light worth saving*

I AM CHARGED WITH POSSESSION OF A FIREARM ON SCHOOL grounds. Dr. Gorum is appealing my case. Meanwhile, I am trying to get readmitted in school. For the duration of my appeals process, two people—Nicole and Dr. Gorum—blessed me with a second chance.

Morgan, my roommate from 2000, referred me to a man he thinks can help me get back in school. Dr. Wendell Gorum is not only the Mass Communications chairman for the college, but also the advisor for the Alpha Phi Alpha fraternity. I quickly learn that he has a superior reputation on campus for being powerful and respected. He agrees to meet with me.

The day I meet Dr. Gorum I am immediately impressed by how seriously he takes me. He sees me as a young man rather than a dangerous gang banger. I explain to him what happened that unfortunate night of December 9. As he takes notes, his body language and expressions put me at ease. He is interested in what I have to say and mentions that he is a huge fan of my talents on the field. He makes a few phone calls to some important faculty members who may be able to help me in my appeal.

With the assistance of Nicole and Dr. Gorum, I prepare the best appeal I can. My appeals process consists of a lot of dedication, footwork, and patience. Like Nicole, Dr. Gorum is a blessing for me because, without Doc, I would have never been allowed to return to school.

I'm informed by one of the committee members, who is also one of my professors, that I'm found to be not responsible. This means that I am not guilty and can return to classes immediately. However, the vice president of the college, Charles Smith, upset that the committee finds me not responsible, overturns the decision. When I receive the letter stating I have to serve a one-year suspension, I'm crushed. I immediately write another appeal to the president of the university because I need to be able to return to school immediately in order to be eligible to compete for my upcoming senior season. I have to have an outstanding senior year to ensure myself a draft pick.

In addition, the committee that initially voted me not responsible is upset that their decision has been changed without their consent. Four of the five members write letters to the president on my behalf, stating the decision to suspend me for one year doesn't reflect their decision.

But many other school officials are upset with me for challenging the VP. Suddenly people's jobs are threatened and I am being blackballed.

While receiving ugly looks, and unfair treatment from the school officials, being expelled from school doesn't impress the NFL.

Once I finally meet with the president and he reviews all the details during my hearings, he grants me a suspension of one semester rather than the entire year. However, there are complications involving my absence in the prior semester. By missing one semester of school, I fall short of the amount of credits required to be eligible to compete in NCAA college football. I'm heartbroken because my senior season is supposed be my meal ticket to the NFL. In addition, there are strict guidelines allowing me back to school. I can't attend any campus events, live in dorms, and am only permitted to be on campus for classes. I'm looked at by the other students and members of my team differently for getting special treatment. I have microscopes on me watching my every move. Still, I'm determined to make my senior year a successful one.

Who would have thought one could receive some of their greatest blessings in life, while dealing with their biggest challenges?

# LETTER FROM MEGGETTE

*Talking to a friend whose way was lost*
*A reply back was never to be received*
*For the dead speaks not*
*I still love*
*Hope is all I possess*
*Hoping these words of tears allow my heart to receive*
*    closure*
*A friend's soul was snatched from me*
*Missing the chance to give my own for you*
*Leaves the pieces of my honor chipping away*
*Memories of the abandoned building we thought to marry*
*    death in*
*If we were only successful that night of our deaths*
*A letter would not be the thorn in my heart*
*These words of love followed by how much I missed*
*Time is to be forever lost*
*Why can't I cope with this pain?*

BEING KICKED OUT OF SCHOOL AND BELIEVING MY NFL DREAMS
are dashed, I don't think my life can get any worse—but it does.
Already at the lowest point in my life, I'll never forget the day I

receive the news. Still in my funk, I am with Nicole helping her at her internship position at a nearby college. It was late at night and just the two of us are in the office. Then, I get a call on my cell phone.

"Machete, Meggette got killed . . . Somebody shot him in the head down the Bity . . ."

I drop the phone and go wild. Devastated and sobbing uncontrollably, I smash my fists into the walls, trash the room, and then fall to the floor, inconsolable. Nicole tries her best to comfort me, but this news breaks me. I'm overwhelmed with grief and guilt.

Months prior, I had received a letter from Meggette:

First, let me start with peace, love, and respect homee. I know by this time you must be really trippin' because you haven't heard from me. First, no matter what you heard about me, as of this moment, it's all lies. I can't begin to explain why I haven't holla'd at you, but I hope that soon we will have a powwow. There are a few things that have been on my mind, Blood. I chose to write this letter bebause it hurts me to see how this brotherhood ended. A lot of things have been going on since you left. I ask myself daily why you left the 'hood. What was out there that you needed that you kouldn't get from the 'hood? When you blooded me in, I thought this shit was fo'eva. I thought we'd B banging fo' life, and CK'z was on site Blood. Have you forgotten all that you taught me and everything we've been through, Blood? All those late nights we risked our lives, Blood. You know after the accident my life changed. I lost my eye, and Kobb didn't make it. I wish I died in that car too.

As far as the rumor that was going on around the 'hood about me saying you and Saint flatted on the 'hood, I didn't mean it like that, Blood. You should know me better than that, and to think I would kick your back in is brazy. While you were away, things got worse for me, bekause I couldn't handle the conditions I was living in anymore. I was living from place to place, and still jux'n to get by, Blood. I contemplated killing myself again a few times, Blood. I left one bullet in the .38 before pulling the trigger. But you wanna know what I kept thinking, "Where the fuck is Machete? Why the fuck am I going through this shit alone, and he is living it up in Delaware?" I was so stressed out about all the changes that took place, I mentioned to a few homees how you flatted on the 'hood, and left your pups stranded, Blood. I resented you for that shit bebause you taught me everything I know, and then you wanted something else out of life at a time when I was still in need. Deep down, I didn't feel like you stranded us, it's just I didn't bee you like I used to, Blood. Shit was a mess on the streets, and I felt a part of me was missing while you were gone. I never imagined you going to kollege, and looking forward to bigger and better things in life. Maybe this was my ignorance but you bred me for one thing and then you changed. I thought the 'hood was it and we'd never leave. I knew we'd eventually meet up and bump heads. I wish I could have done it over and just called you to tell you how I felt. Now I understood why you sent the homees at me. I'm sure it hurt you just as much as it hurt me, but you had to look out for the set. It hurt me deeply to see the homees come at me like that, but I understood. I disappointed myself, for allowing it to come to this. You know I'm a better man than that, but the 'hood took me under. I always knew gang bangin' would be the death of me, just like we planned, remember? I know I brought this on myself. Until we meet again, dub side.

This is the last communication between Meggette and me. He is killed before I'm ready to respond to this letter. To this day, I suffer the unbearable weight of guilt, for my conscience will not rest regarding his death. Now, the person I considered my best friend is gone. I feel partly responsible for it and every day I wish I answered him before it was too late. I would have told him . . .

Wass hannin' Blood? Pardon my soul for not responding to your letter. Overlooking the rumor was something I couldn't do. That shit had Blood tight, hearing all those crazy-ass rumors Blood. You know how da streets talk, so what was I suppose to do? You were my ace nigga, now we beefing? Nah Blood, I still got love for you homee. Why couldn't you get at me so we could've squashed dat shit? You know I would never abandon you Blood, but I had to make changes in my life. I still got love for you homee till da cradle. On Piru, you know I love you homee. P-Funk, off the toP Soo Woo BlXXd.

What hurts most about his death is we never got an opportunity to make amends. It hurts even more when I have to face his mom, Rita, who's practically down with the set. When I come home right after his death, I visit Rita. I prepare myself to deal with her condition. Once I get into Orange, I stop at the liquor store to buy a 40-oz hoping to lose all feeling for what I'm heading into. Facing the mother of a homee who's just been murdered ain't easy. Turning left on Parrow Street, I head straight to 108 projects where she lives. Pulling up to the building, it's clear mourners have visited Rita before me. There's a gathering in front of the building where homees from East and West Side sets collaborate on revenge. Only this time, the enemy is Blood. Unlike what most people believe, on the East Coast, there is more Blood-on-Blood killings than Blood vs. Crip.

• • •

Before entering the apartment, I greet homees with gangster shakes, and down some Ru juice. Homees have clearly been faded by his death. After three knocks on the rusty project door, Rita opens it with a look of "will you just shoot me dead right here." We embrace immediately while she cries and shouts repeatedly for God to bring her baby back. I lead her toward the couch so she can sit and regain her composure. A few homees already in the apartment help me to console Rita. After getting herself together, Rita invites me into Meggette's room where there lies a .25 automatic, two red flags, and some Blood literature. She says that he would want me to have them. At the same time I can't help but notice how aged she looks.

She adds that she needs a drink and she wants to get out of the house. I agree and lead her back outside to the G-ride.

In search of some much needed alcohol, we end up at Brandy's on Park Street. Inside, she takes shot after shot while talking to Meggette as if he's next to her. We toast a few drinks, and then she finally asks me, "What do I do now, Dae? They took my son and now what the fuck do I do. Please tell me."

I don't know what to say but I know something needs to be said. "Rita, I am sorry, what do you want me to do?" I already know what she is thinking. By now, her anger overtakes her sadness as she hostilely demands me to find and decapitate that son of a bitch who killed her baby. We already know who's responsible.


Once I hit the street, I'm on patrol for this nigga. I know him from my block where we sold drugs together, G is a Blood. But now I intend to send him to hell. Day in and day out I patrol the streets hoping and praying to find him. I know I'll catch his ass slippin'. At night I replay how Meggette got murdered.

*"Machete, Meggette got killed . . . Somebody shot him in the head down the Bity"* sounds off in my head throughout the day. I can't seem to shake the violent image of him laid out on the pavement.

Meggette's wake is the hardest thing for me to face. The night before, Saint, Ace, Derrick, Mu, and I stay up all night getting his BIP shirts prepared.

Before going to the church, I drive by the spot where he was murdered. As I pass by, the vision of his brains splattered all over the pavement replays in my mind over and over again like a scene from a horror movie.

Stepping inside the church, I can hear the sound of an organ playing. It's the same sad song that I hear at every funeral. A few relatives faint and some have to be restrained from grabbing the casket. My head starts feeling light. My mind slips into another world. The homees are bick'n'it with a few Pirettes who show some emotional compassion.

I can't even fix my eyes on him. I'm in hell. Although music is playing, I can't hear it. My world is in total silence as I flat-line toward his coffin. The closer I get to the casket the more the tears swim uncontrollably down my face. I try to mentally brace myself for the inevitable feelings. The shock, the tears, the anxiety, and the bottomless love making me want to trade places with my nigga. The heartache and pain I feel since I lost him intensifies ten times as I look down at him in the box.

Standing in front of the casket, my legs feel shaky and the lights seem to brighten. The crowd in attendance around me starts to blur. I close my eyes and zone off . . . *Why the fuck you leave me Blood, what the fuck am I suppose to do without—?* My moment is interrupted by Saint's arrival next to me. He stands beside me with a desperate gaze while the rest of the 'hood files behind him, just like the Marines. Looking at the cushioned casket and li'l homee's face, the room slowly begins to whirl around. All the good times come rollin' up on my mental screen. My knees grow weaker and my eyes dampen. Not only because he is dead, but also because of the status of our friendship before he is killed. Knowing who killed my nigga, his name echoes in my head over and over until I become furious. *I'm a kill dat nigga, I'm a kill his mama, I'm a kill his baby's mama. Whoever I catch him wit, they're good as dead too.* I close my eyes and picture Meggette, his pimp shades he used to wear, the first ride we went on, and our suicide attempt. The nights we talked about personal things outside of bangin', like what we wanted to be in life or where would we live if we could move tomorrow. We talked about finding wives, getting married, and having kids in the future. It's talks like these that I miss the most because, deep down, he wanted out of the lifestyle. While in the midst of my thoughts, I feel Saint's arm embrace me with a hug that strips me of all my strength. I'm completely weak and vulnerable. *Nigga iz gon' bleed fo' this.*

People continually pour into the church to view Meggette's body as cries and shouts to the heavens above ring throughout. I reach out and touch his hand. His flesh is cold and unreal. *I know you can feel me.* The tears begin.

"I'm sorry Blood." I wait for as long as the people behind me can be patient to hear his response, but silence persists. Gazing at his body, I know that he is no longer there. Whatever force and power that breathed life into him has vanished. Death is supposed to be an ending, but not for me, it's the beginning of an intolerable hell. We had frequent talks about death and I thought I had come to terms with it, but his death has suddenly assumed an unwanted reality.

Finally I bend over the casket, place a light kiss on his forehead, and whisper to him, "I got chu Blood, dat nigga dead. I love you, Blood funk fo'eva," then I lose all feeling, for his flesh isn't soothing.

They've done a lot of work on my homee for him to have an open casket. Meggette is sewn together like a stuffed rag doll, considering he took six to his mental.

The set sits at the back of the room, all dressed down wearing shirts with a picture of Meggette on them. I give his mom a shirt but I receive one of the coldest vibes I have ever received. She accepts it, but the chemistry isn't the same. I feel deep down, she believes I am responsible for her son's death.

Family and friends repeatedly tell me, "Be strong." Homees swearing, "It's on, Blood. We gon' paint the town red," but for me, the words have little impact.

While sitting in my seat listening to the pastor read the Bible, I get a strange feeling that someone is watching me. When I glance up, I spot Rita looking at me with disappointment and a puzzled face that seems to ask the question, "How could you let this happen to my baby?" I think this is the first time I have ever lowered my head in disgust and shame. I don't know what to say to Rita.


Sometimes I think I suffer just as much as he did. Still do. Sometimes I think that he's the winner and I'm the loser. I still claw my way out of nightmares all these years later; and I will continue to years from now. I don't want to forget. I don't think I should. I still cry. I see myself in the nightmare. I see myself following his footsteps that day. I can't see the face of the gunman. I ask him to pull the trigger. I beg him to send me to Meggette. He won't fire. I still exhale, blowing the images of him in that casket out of my mind's eye.

Nightmares torment me. Horrific, unrelenting, full of gunfire, death, and eternal darkness. Fearsome visions plague my sleep every night. This is the price I have to pay for my history of violence. There is no mercy.

# HELL'Z KITCHEN

*A place no one would like to call home*
*But I dwell here*
*Shortening my every breath and step*
*I've become the place I hate the most*
*I now know why I hate myself*

AFTER MY SECOND YEAR OF PLAYING COLLEGE FOOTBALL, I
continue to spark interest from the NFL. I achieve what no one
at the program has ever done. I am literally and statistically one
of the most dangerous assets college football produces this year,
and I receive a lot of attention from NFL scouts. As a result of my
hard work, I'm named Black College All-American and to the
First-Team All-American list leading the country in kick returns
for touchdowns with three for 800 yards off twenty-three returns.
I did this over the course of five games. After the fifth game, opponents wouldn't kick the ball to me anymore. I also racked up 1,450
all-purpose yards, ranking in the top ten in the nation. My success
on the field generates so much national media attention, ranging
from ESPN to the Associated Press, I know the NFL is just a step
away.

Camron, a scout player, stands like a fan as he watches me do my thing. His contributions to the team are not on the same level as mine.

On two different occasions, he puts on a show of disrespect by lashing out at me, "You fag, you bitch." His words sting like acid on my flesh. How can I accept this from a busta whose life is worth less than the ants I walk on?

Trying to do the right thing in the civilian world sometimes means tolerating the wrong things in mine. In my world you don't walk away from a challenge. If someone steps on your shoes without a convincing apology, violence has to follow. Despite my recent progress, I still can't overlook what most will. After years of living in a culture unknown to most people, I drag my secret world front and center at college. Now my worlds are expected to operate in tandem.

My civilizations begin bleeding out of my ass for they both want rights of ownership. Knowing I can't get involved in any disturbances given that clemency has been granted once, I gaze at Camron with the hope that he'll see the fire in my eyes, the fury burning from my soul.

*B, do you really believe you can match up against me? I'm Machete, the nigga that be serving mothafuckas gladly. Not a fucking chance. Why play this game you have no intention of finishing? Fool fronting like I won't fund him a trip to hell. You know, front-page his ass. But fuck it, since you handed in your first payment, I'll definitely make the last, I'm always down to play. Trust and believe, you'll see.*

If he would just heed the message, he won't have to find out the hard way. Why can't he see this? What part of my character signifies weakness? But I eventually figure it out; I know why he feels compelled to challenge me. It's simple; it's the male ego, pride, and the idea that he has to defend himself against competition.

I am already depressed for failing to take advantage of my opportunity with the NFL a few weeks earlier. Getting caught with a gun in my room caused every NFL scout that came to visit me to be alarmed instead of admiring.

"Are you in a gang, Mr. Morris?"

"Why did you have a gun in your room?"

"Why should we take a chance on you?"

I shake my head and will myself not to reveal my anger in regard to their questions. I summon every ounce of energy stored in my mind and body not to say "Fuck y'all, you think you can do this to me?"

Before my final, pivotal encounter with Camron, I'm in the process of getting a better understanding of the person I am. *Why did I even come to college?* I came on the faith that once I finished, I would be in the NFL and could financially take care of my family and my 'hood. It seems that the more I hold back, the more Camron insults me. The thought of him having the upper hand is something that I am not familiar with. At this point, my demons kick in, and the idea of killing Camron or just walking away is like a tug-of-war pulling back and forth on my mind.

After several bouts of this fool mouthing off at me, I'm like a bomb ready to explode. I finally catch up with Camron when he least expects it.

It's sometime around 11:00 P.M. and the college's Greek clubs are cooking out on their respective lawns, essentially hangout spots for grilling and stepping. Sponsored and funded by the school's administration, the Greek clubs are well respected throughout the campus. It's common to catch the Greeks on their lawns entertaining prospects with prerehearsed steps and roll calls.

I am hanging with O, Naz, and K-Blok in the midst of this good groove, nodding my head to "Good Times" by Styles P. I'm lost in thought about my current misfortunes; my gaze is abruptly broken by the sound of a familiar voice.

"Yo, you good?"

Piecing the voice and the face together, a smile emerges from my face followed by a nod. "Uh-huh."

K-Blok tosses a cold one at me, and then fakes a jab to my jaw. "Ease up a bit. Don't let that shit spoil ya night." He has no clue what is on my mind but my body language must have told him I was upset.

Buzzing off the vibes of the music and the sangria already in my system, revenge tiptoes its way into my train of thought as I spot a familiar figure to my left entering. Wiping the creases of my eyes to get a quick confirmation I recognize him: Camron. He and his homee are in the middle of an animated conversation, unaware of anything around them—cardinal sin, straight slippin'. Perfect!

I make my move.

Melodramatic as it may sound, getting laid that night by two European models would have been runner-up in what I desired most right then. The satisfaction I needed lay with Camron. I have this bad habit of allowing my misery to take control of me. Hungry and willing, I become oblivious to all people and time around me. I'm completely zoned the fuck out. My mind is fully focused on my immediate plan, which I intend to complete with perfection.

Now fully on the prowl, my mouth begins to water as my pupils dilate. There's turbulence within me I can barely contain. I feel my waist to make sure I have my baby. "Time's up mothafucka." Sizing him up like a leopard hunting a gazelle before I discreetly slip away from the crowd, I discard all regard for life, what is right, who gets hurt, and ultimately my future.

Naz and O are in support of my attack. Naz is a civilian I get down with from Camden. He is always down to ride out if I need him, plus his 285 pounds are added insurance to control just about any physical situation I can't handle.

"Wess happ'nin' Blood?" I shout with enough air to fill both cheeks when Blood is articulated.

Camron and his homee stare back at me, revealing their nervousness and surprise while my eyes speak the repressed hate built up inside me. *Why the fuck cats be pinning their tails between they legs when shit's bout to pop?*

Without further delay, I flash my baby machete I always carry and his entire body convulses in a shudder of terror. As for his clone, he feels the heat of the blade as his eyes tell his story: *What did I do, I ain't got nothing to do with this!*

Giving me a lost look, Camron solicits, "Wassup, what's goin' on?" in a thin flat voice that tries to sound friendly. I can't identify this tone, so it takes me a second to connect.

I let out a monstrous laugh.

*"You know what's goin' on and why I'm here."*

His eyes search mine for any signs of mercy, trying to fool me, but behind the wide-open gaze is an animal caught in headlights.

Now on a level playing field, I take the opportunity to invite him into my world. This stupid mothafucka doesn't even know I've served so many fools, I'm rich off just tips alone, and I am all too happy to supply his meal *on the house.* How could he not recognize I'm a bona fide threat to society?

"M . . . Ma . . . Machete—, I ain't got no problem wit chu, I— I ain't know it was that serious."

*Huh!* I think as I am rendered speechless.

His comeback resonates in the air between us, forcing me to think, *Okay let's back up and pretend like that didn't happen.*

For two seconds, I feel like a judge handing down the death penalty, exercising the power of life and death, and Camron is reluctant to tempt my anger. Considering I waited for this opportunity far too long, ICU is where I intend to send him.

Camron sighs as I settle into the groove of my B-Dawg stance; diminishing his street image before everyone is just an added satisfaction, more thrilling before the takedown.

His weakness accelerates my lack of sympathy as I take liberty in doubling up a combo to his jaw, shank still in hand, as he falls to the ground. After he falls, everything seems to slow down, which is odd because in the past, everything seemed to move fast at the point of impact. This time is different; a delicious tension envelops us. I feel a sweet anticipating thrill as I repeatedly puncture his flesh. I can feel the steel slide through him, scraping bone. Through all the repressed anger, the hate I have for life, my pessimism toward the future, and this busta I can't stand, I enjoy every moment. With every punch and swing of the blade, I feel relief in his anguish.

In my peripheral vision I spot Naz and O serving his comrade. Naz is testing his knuckle game while O struggles for leverage to deliver more skull-crushing blows with his size 12 Timberlands. I hear them competing for bragging rights about who rendered the most damage. "Man, did you see how hard I hit him? I think I broke my fuckin' hand." Spectators materialize from everywhere in a matter of seconds. I swell in ecstasy, for my pent-up desires have finally come true. After each sizzling strike, his pleas are like music to my ears.

Just as I imagined, he starts begging and pleading, hands shielding his face. "I don't wanna fight!" Breathing heavily, whimpering and bitching, "Stop! Chill! Please!"

I strike even harder. "Man the fuck up nigga."

His screams border between panic and absolute terror leaving echoes vibrating through the night.

He stumbles for cover as the bystanders watch with fear on their faces. He's still able to walk away, so I charge after him, stabbing him again in the back and triceps as he falls over the railing.

"Sooo mothafuckin' WooP nigga, hold dat mothafucka!" I shout, getting off on the echoes that vibrate from building to building as I stand over him, in victory above his weakened and Bloody body. I jog to the car and go home.

Camron reports the incident to the police. By now I have downed a 40-oz, and stash the shank at K-Blok's apartment. Moments later, my phone rings—it's Naz.

"Yo Machete, this fool ova here telling. He told 'em you stab—"

I cut in: "Yo! Yo! Be easy on the jack homez they floating."

"Ri-right, my bad, where you at?"

Weighing the options of his question, I retort, "I'm good homee, I'll get back at chu on that, but where you at?"

"Same spot, but cho B, this nigga squealing, fuck you wanna do about this shit?"

"Just chill the fuck out and keep an eye out Blood."

"You already know, just lay low B."

"Fasho, good lookin' Blood, later."

"Later."

Knowing the boys will be after me, I decide to turn myself in since I ain't one for much running.

Once I step into the station, I'm immediately taken into custody and interrogated for four hours. I'm arrested and charged with first-degree assault and transported to Delaware's correctional center in Smyrna. Bail is set at $10,000.

Since this constitutes the first time I've been incarcerated, it now hits me that I am far from home and have no idea of who is in this prison I had a beef with. The irony of my arrest is that I have been an immaculate criminal in my past ten years. After dodging the system for so long, I felt untouchable. But all good things must come to an end. In speaking about doing time, when you live the life of a banger, prison is a mandatory pit stop f reputable criminal.

All sorts of questions begin rushing through my mind. Can I hold up in prison? Can I humble myself to become accustomed to prison? Will some hotshot try me? Shit, I will be the new fish and we all know what that means. Will I lose my temper and have to ice a mothafucka or will I be the one getting my toe tagged?

While incarcerated, I start to think about the people who matter most to me, my family. Neina stands strong with me. I feel strength knowing she's on the outside working with me. I feel security with her as crazy as that sounds. As the voices inside my head begin to scream, I have no answers.

*You're a fuckin' loser! How did you end up in this situation?*

In my cell, the bed is hard as bricks; mattresses are no bigger than the width of my shoulders. The sink and toilet are connected and both reek with the brutal exhaust of defecation, urine, and who knows what else. Lying in this filthy cell at night is the most difficult time of the day because there is nowhere to run and hide, just me, my thoughts, and a cellie. With this first-degree assault charge pending, my life is at a low point. I simply can't imagine my life getting worse.

Fortunately for me, I will only remain on the inside for three days before posting bail. After bailing out, I make sure I stay under the radar. I move cautiously around campus. Evidence is lined up against me, and I know one more infraction will bury me on the assault alone.

With my assault charge pending, I'm expelled from the university for the second time.

On June 1, 2004, my situation gets progressively worse because once again I'm arrested on campus.

The beef with the Bloods and the football team has reached a peak of bangin' on sight. My homee O from the Bronx got jumped by an entourage of football players at the request of the ringleader, James. The beef is stemming from a falling out between James and me. We are both wide receivers. During my first two years at the university we grow to be tight. We travel together as designated partners where we collaborate on ideas for the following day's challenge.

While our natural positions bond us, hidden agendas divide us. In the midst of trying to get reinstated in 2002 after getting evicted for possession of a firearm, James's true colors surface with two snake heads.

Justin, one of the team captains, circulates a petition in an attempt to convince the university to reconsider my expulsion. While this occurs, rumors fly that James is in favor of my expulsion, and more important, wants to keep me out of school. When the petition is signed by my teammates and ready to be submitted, one name is left off—James.

James and my homee O get into beef in the cafeteria that leaves O badly beaten by James and his associates. Word gets back to me that a Blood was jumped in the cafeteria.

My homee Justin from Harlem, New York, and I set out to confront James at his apartment.

Standing face-to-face in James's doorway, we exchange heated words. He claims there was no jumping, just a fair fight. I consider poppin' his ass on sight right now, but then what? I'll go on the run for murder. So I play it cool and assemble my hand in the form of a gun. I point it directly at his face before sounding, "Boom!"

A few days after our confrontation, I want James gone. All I think about is looking him in his eyes in his last moments before I send him to his maker.

Soon after, James gets into another fight with my homees.

One thing leads to another and gunshots fly.

A former teammate, Will, is shot six times. I am arrested and charged with first-degree attempted murder, conspiracy to commit murder, possession of a gun, and rioting.

My daughter is due to be born in a couple weeks.

I'm the prime suspect because the victim alleges that while he is being assaulted by as many as twenty individuals, most of them wearing burgundy flags, he hears me order the unknown assailant to shoot him. In the victim's statement, it reads, "Machete ordered that Blood to shoot me. I heard him say, 'Buss 'em, buss 'em.'" With these additional allegations, the Dover police have enough to book me again. I'm jailed and given a $165,000 bail.

When I get locked up for the attempted murder, two detectives question me on the shooting. During the interrogation, they make it clear Bloods are not welcome in Delaware.

Grabbing me up by my collar and throwing me into a chair, the detective challenges: "Listen you fuckin' gang bangin' punk, we don't do that shit here!"

"This is a true blue state, keep that shit in Jersey."

"All you mothafuckas do is terrorize innocent people, and fight over colors."

"Y'all are a bunch of punks who hide behind rags."

I cut in by saying, "You don't know shit mothafu—"

Immediately I am lifted up by my collar. "You think you tough nigger!" This cop is so close to my face, I feel showers coming from his mouth with every word he speaks. His partner hovers over me, clearly waiting for the green light to begin a good old-fashioned ass whooping. By now, any bad moves on my part will initiate what they want to do.

Detective Tarila tears open a pack of gum and tosses a stick in his mouth. "Where's the shooter, Mr. Morris?"

They start bombarding me simultaneously with a lot of different questions in hopes that they will confuse me or get me to con-tradict myself. At times during the interrogation they make threats to beat me senseless. They want me to give a written statement con-cerning the part I played in the shooting. First of all, I'm not about to say anything that is self-incriminating. I didn't do it when I had been questioned by the detectives for stabbing Camron. I play the dumb "I don't know anything" role until they get tired of me.

"I want a lawyer."

"Look we can play hardball or we can make this easier on the both of us, give me a name."

My eyes glint, the trade-off of snitching and freedom sucks.

"You know, Mr. Morris, we know you are not the shooter but you damn sure know who did it so give us what we want."

"We have witnesses placing you at the scene."

A muscle in my cheek flexed. Detective Tarila studied me for a long moment. Then he nodded to his partner while tearing off a scrap of blank paper and slowly sliding it across the table to me.

"Write down what happened from beginning to end."

Now self-preservation kicks in as I think of my options. Snitch-ing is out of the question, so what the hell am I to do? Detective Tarila even has the nerve to try and tie Bloods into a murder that took place on campus, another stabbing of a Blood, and a few other crimes in Dover.

"We know you had something to do with Champ's murder too, so here's your chance to help yourself."

"We got statements placing the Bloods at the scene, and you as the leader."

I know this is bullshit because if they really had tips on me, they would have been looking for me. These guys figure, Let's try and squeeze some additional information out of this nigga because he is already fucked.

So once again I state, "I want a lawyer."

. . .

Now I am in Pre-Trial, awaiting a trial date. I can't make bail.

Delaware Correctional Center contains nine Security Housing Units, SHU, which are divided into tiers. There are two- and three-man cells, and single cells for prison workers. The prison is bordered by nothing but woods and country with the gun towers eclipsing everything from the inside.

The SHU houses inmates who cannot be kept in a lesser security setting and/or whose behavior and history are conducive to maximum-security housing. In addition, inmates sentenced to the death penalty are housed in a unit called S-1. There are three hundred cells there. Each cell is single-bunked. Inmates in the SHU are locked in their cells twenty-three hours a day. They can use their one hour out of their cell to shower and exercise.

The Maximum Housing Unit, MHU, is a step down from the SHU and a step up from the general population. The MHU has 588 beds in 300 cells.

Pre-Trial consists of inmates who have not been convicted. They are housed in their own building, which is more laid-back and has more privileges and allows more movement than other units.

The first night, I lay awake, filled with loneliness and a feeling of regret.

Filing out of my cell heading to chow, I stand behind a shorter inmate, and in front of a taller one. Ear hustling some prison talk in my rear, I recognize a familiar voice. I turn around and see my homee Taz. "Wass up Blood?" he says. Taz is a Blood; he's from 93 Gangsters, and awaiting trial on first-degree murder charges.

Meeting up with Taz is a relief. No one wants to be alone and outnumbered in an unfamiliar place, let alone prison, so reuniting with him puts me at ease. Taz is from the Bronx, and moved to Delaware a few months earlier for legal reasons. Taz's situation is more serious than mine because he and another homee got bagged for a body in Manchester. Manchester is one of the rougher neighborhoods in Dover, so everyone from that neighborhood has in some way, shape, or form been victimized by Blood. Taz practically runs the joint, putting fear in many of the inmates' hearts before he ever opens his mouth.

We are both in Pre-Trial, I'm on C-Tier for attempted murder, and he's on B-Tier for murder. He sends me kites through the laundry man.

Immediately in Pre-Trial, I rip off a piece of my T-shirt; spark it up with Piru Glyphics. One shirt reads "Newark," another "P-Funk," and another "Banged Up."

In one of Taz's kites, he tells me about an inmate adversary on my tier he's been waiting to stab. Somewhere in the letter I anticipate reading something to the effect of him telling me to poke the fool up. But there is no mention of that. He wants the nigga to himself but I take a position on the matter myself. I live by the G-code. Beef with mines, then the beef is mines. The letter reads:

Homee, you watch yo self over there BeBause dez niggaz is BraBBz. They hate Blood, and given the chance to wash us out, they might take it. Right now our numbers are low in here as far as damus go, but we have a few dedickated soldiers. We got an Inglewood Family on A-Tier named Blurk; he got knokked off in town in a drug raid. Over in Wiktor Building, we got a Tree Top homee from Vegas named B, Nimrod from G.K.B. in 3rd letter building, and a 104 CMG homee from St. Louis named Lane. There's Tech from 93 too, he's one of my breeds. There's a few more floating around, but these are the reckognized homees. So these kats know we put it down, but keep your window open Blood, and I'll mail some metal to you through my laundry man. There is also a hand full of Sur 13s in here from Kali too, and we already got into it with them tacKo eatin mothafucKa's. So tucK this missile Buzz C/O's B Shaking down. Until the RED moon howls stay 050, and stay Banged up. Eaaa555 to the we555 B7XXd.

Considering the amount of my bail, I know I'll be in prison until I'm sentenced. By now, I'm feeling sick to my stomach, and thoughts of not getting out drive me crazy.

I find it impossible to be excited by the imminent birth of my daughter, who is due in two weeks. I try to convince myself not to love her for fear of my not being there. I don't want to drag Neina and the baby into this prison bid. I have to handle it myself.

Sitting on an attempted murder among other charges in the state of Delaware, along with the reputation I have, is no joke. They are known for burying jokers for the weakest charges. I've seen them give a nigga 120 days for a nickel bag of weed that wasn't even found in his possession. In Newark, New Jersey, a cop will either do one of two things: stomp on your shit, or keep it and smoke it himself.

During my pretrial stay, I summon up my entire life. How, where, and when did my life take such a bad turn? Will my daughter grow up as a bastard? I weigh my unfortunate circumstances, them having me, and me not having her.

The only time I find the slightest peace of mind in the joint is at the yard. I hit the dip and do pull-ups on the bar, while I place my mind in a comfort zone. There's something about working out that relieves you, or at least for me it did. Once again, it's when the night falls that I gasp for air, my eyes tear up, and my fists clench as I deliver blow after blow to my cell wall. With sleepless nights, as my thoughts ricochet inside my head, it is only the sound of the C/O shouting, "Chowww, first call for chowww," that brings me back to reality. Looking back at the whole period, I never felt so small, so powerless, so weak, exposed, and humiliated before or since.

Lying in my bed flashing back over the events in question, my bunkie, who's in on attempted murder charges as well, makes his way off the top bunk to take a leak. Either his age or his health tells me his physical condition because the drop seems too much for his bones as he grunts and groans immediately after landing. This is clearly not the first time he's been down because the room is decorated like a lavish home. He converts his whole world into his cell.

Sometime later, while staring out my cell window, he asks in a concerned and curious voice, "Why are you so angry?"

After a second or two of digesting his strange question, I respond, "Because I'm in here, we ain't at Disneyland, we in prison."

If hate, depression, and rage are colors, then I'm a clown. Ol' head asks again, but this time with obvious hopes that I'll go into my situation. Not really up for much conversation, I still choose to hear him out. He goes on to explain how a lot of us younger generation criminals love to do the crime, but hate doing the time. After calculating his words, the rational part of my brain says there is truth to his words, but my heart says, *Fuck what you talking about.*

Ol' head and I speak about a lot, as I start to ponder my actions in this whole ordeal.

● ● ●

During my second week in prison, I make a phone call to Mom. She picks up on the first ring and the smile that has been suppressed for days slides across my face. The happiness I feel at the sound of her voice is like the joy of a father holding his first child. It's beyond words. "Hi baby!"

She isn't taking this situation too well and will probably end up drinking again. She says many things to me within the ten-minute call, but to hear her hurt over the phone sends painful chills through me.

She's a nervous wreck. In the conversation, she blames herself for my problems, saying over and over through endless tears, "What did I do? Where did I go wrong?" Her pain and guilt leave me feeling helpless.

My mother says, "Dashaun, I've tried my best to raise you and your brother the best I could. I don't know what I did wrong. I always ask myself how and when I lost you and your brothers. Both of you have turned from my little baby boys into animals or something, and I don't know what else to do. I can't take this anymore."

I interrupt Mama because I can't handle another word. The more she reflects the more it hurts. "Mom, I love you; it's not your fault. You did all that you could." After hearing the operator bust through, "You have one minute remaining for this conversation," I banged the phone up against the wall out of frustration.

Mom interjected, "Dashaun, please try to calm down, I need for you to tell me you will be okay. I need to know you ain't gon' try to hurt yourself. Please promise me!"

At night, I replay our conversation over and over in my head as the tears mix with my anger and empathy for my mother. I punch the wall over and over and over until I'm exhausted and Blood pours through my fingers dripping to the floor.

After another week in, my family comes to visit. I sit in my seat restlessly trying to hold my anxiety level in check as I wait to see

Neina's lovely face and my mother's. The moment Neina turns the corner, I notice she is as lovely as ever. Our eyes lock with an intensity that could have melted me whole. Our conversation is dictated by reality, and the reality of my dire situation is that I'm not going anywhere anytime soon. Up and down the gloomy visiting row, the same game plays itself out: the women are looking for words of encouragement, something from their spouses that signifies things will be okay, something that will give them a sign of hope to hold on to. But there is very little to be had.

Later on that night, I lie in bed drifting over thoughts and ideas, all the time thinking, How am I going to get out of here?

To my surprise, I manage to post bail.

Two days after I get home, I'm heading to the hospital. This is the place where life begins and ends. Going in I am nervous, I don't know what to expect or how to act and react. I know something big is going down; my first child, Da-Shana, is about to be born and I know I have to be there to support Neina. I have to be strong. After experiencing so much death, for the first time in my life I am about to witness birth in the flesh.

With every moment the intensity of the situation rises. I feel tingly inside, almost compelled to leave. It's like some supernatural shit is happening. I hold the camera as steady as I can, while still trying to take a peak at what's happening in living color. Suddenly I notice a head pop up, and my knees get weak; my stomach turns.

The nurses are in full work mode, no laughs, hurling aggressive demands at each other while Neina keeps pushing. I don't know my place. I don't know what to do. Right now all the worries of the streets don't mean shit to me. I have only one concern: my baby girl, my li'l homee, the one I am now responsible and obligated to be there for, unconditionally. The nurse pulls out a vacuum and sucks her out by her head.

I don't like the way this looks. I think they are hurting her so I cut in, "What are you doing? You hurting her?"

"Please, sir, we know what we're doing. I'll need for you to step aside; she is fine," says Dr. Kahn.

Reluctantly, I follow the doctor's orders and watch, helplessly from the side. A few more minutes and she's here. They scoop mucus out of her eyes, nose, and mouth; it's nasty. I hear the first sound of her little voice as she cries, announcing her arrival. They dangle her around while Neina lay exhausted, in total awe at the sight of the life she just brought into the world.

After they clean up my daughter, they put her in our arms. As I hold her for the first time, I feel submissive to her every need. It's not about me anymore. This is the first time I feel like I am in control of something. I realize in this moment that I am not wrecking a life; I created a new life, my own flesh and blood. I handle her with so much care. I feel weird, a little weak and soft. It's all good though; it's worth it.

I immediately fall in love with her skin tone, her smell, and her fingers and toes. Putting the icing on the cake, Da-Shana finally opens her eyes—damn! She is the most precious and gorgeous miracle on earth. How can I let her down, not provide stability for her? I have to and I will. Gazing into her deep brown eyes, I whisper, "Wass hannin' li'l mama? It's Daddy. I love you."

I watched Da-Shana enter this world and, in her, I see myself, my future. With her birth I, too, am reborn. As she opened her eyes, the veil of ignorance, self-hatred, and reckless selfishness was lifted from mine. My eyes are now open, along with hers, with a whole new vision and value for my life. She sparks my will to live; I want to live for her. I don't want to forfeit all my years of watching her grow. So I have to switch up my program, begin taking control of my life, and make something of myself that she and I can both be proud of. This is my commitment to her and to myself. This is the message I'm taking to the streets. They can't claim my life anymore. They didn't get me in the past seventeen years and they can't have me now, for I am a man on a mission.

I have little hope of getting out of this jam. I can't see voluntarily walking into a courtroom to get sentenced. Especially when so-called street cats bend, twist, and violate the rules. The shit seems unfair to a nigga like me who is now the victim for obliging the street code.

Once word touches back home, my homees already know what they have to do, for snitching is ground rules for immediate dismissal.

Talking to Jay from Harlem, New York, he reminds me, "Dae, you know if you lose this case, they gon' bury you?"

"I know Blood," I blurt out. "I'm fucked up right now."

"On Blood, these snitches gotta go," Jay offers.

I pause for a moment, considering my options. "I hear you Blood, but something tells me that ain't gon' change shit." It wasn't too long ago that I would have been thinking along the same lines, sending troops out, and it wouldn't have been a conversation about it except deciding when and where. Jay tries to convince me to kill the snitch. Call it exhaustion or just plain old not giving a fuck, because at that point, I didn't give a damn how it turned out. Mental exhaustion is by far more demeaning than physical for I needed time to get ahold of the situation.

"Yo, the nigga violated B, he gotta go!" He pauses to size up my reaction to the impact of his words.

Now staring him directly in his eyes I say, "Is you berious Blood, this is a commonwealth state. If we lay this fool down, I think the state gon' still pick up the case, but now with added reason to throw my ass in jail."

I had no clue about commonwealth states, or for that matter

what the hell commonwealth meant. But from what I heard in the past, Delaware prosecutes, and sentences, extra hard.

"Tell me what's your plan then?" His tone seems irritated, and a bit sarcastic.

"Actually, I don't have a plan; I'll have to fight it. They are all over me, sweating me like a sauna, and now to invite some new heat ain't good.

"Blood, I'ma need to bang this one around a few more times," I say with uncertainty.

If I want to fight this, I know the only way I have a chance is through a high-paid attorney. I consult with my mother and we decide to pool our finances to see how much help we can afford.

My family ends up hiring Joe Hurley, an attorney based in Wilmington, Delaware. A few days after our initial conversation, I meet with Hurley at his office. He comes highly recommended by an associate who says he is one of the top lawyers in Delaware.

On our first visit, we are ushered into his office and greeted by a gaunt, scholarly looking man of fifty-something years. He has snow-white hair; broad, singularly bony shoulders; an expression of dreary humor; and a plain, strong face upon which stress has left its indelible mark, as if to say "I am getting too old for this shit." Blue-eyed, conservative professional. He welcomes us to some fine Poland Spring water, which is far from my preferred tap water, and a firm handshake.

During the ensuing hour, I brief him on the incident. He jots down everything I say without saying much of anything back. I feel a bit more confident about his authority as I observe various newspaper articles, plaques, and awards for outstanding work hanging everywhere. Interviews with Diane Sawyer, ABC, NBC, and many others send chills of hope through me. *If anybody can get me out of this jam, he can.*

When the meeting is finally over, he gives a peculiar sigh before saying, "I'll need a few days to investigate this, and I'll get back to you." I try to get a take on him by his body language but this dude is straight-up business. He has his game face on and I can't tell whether he believes me, or just wants my retainer's fee.

We eventually retain Hurley, Joe as he told us to call him, paying $5,000 up front and $8,500 thereafter. During the next eleven months, I attend court countless times. The appearances consist of a preliminary hearing, an indictment, a case review, a final case review, and the possibility of a trial. It's all out of your hands, and your life depends on the mood, intelligence, and power of another mothafucka. At this point in time, shit is looking bad for me. Two witnesses have given statements saying they recall hearing me shout "Buss 'em, buss 'em!" This, in addition to the victim's statement, discredits anything and everything I have to say. I dread every trip down the turnpike as I read the hideous-looking sign, "Welcome to Delaware."

One year later at my final case review, Joe informs me that a plea has been proposed. It consists of accepting a riot and assault third-degree charge. I'm facing first-degree attempted murder, first-degree assault, conspiracy to commit murder, rioting, and possession of a firearm. I'm facing twenty-five years in jail, and an infant baby girl who needs me. Damn!

My family and I think long and hard about the plea deal offered by the prosecutor. I go over the pros and cons of the plea again and again in my mind. Joe leaves the decision up to me.

# EXPENSIVE LESSONS

*Emerging from a world's discuss*
*Disgusting a truth within*
*A mask over GOD's light*
*Proudly I wore*
*For a zoo cage is now to be called home*
*Steel were the bars to soften a man's spirit*
*Cold were the bars that turn my child's heart of ice*
*Friends may alter their shades*
*For what was once gold appears bronze*
*A time's escape is loves depreciated*
*Men of mistakes cost ones of love dearly*
*Paying dearly I know best*

---

THE DAY BEFORE MY SENTENCING JAY THROWS ME A SURPRISE going-away party. The event turns out to be an emotional night for us all. The homees have all written promise letters to me detailing what they pledge to me while I'm gone. They express how they feel about me, certified Blood love. I can't believe all the deep emotions they reveal in their letters.

Sitting in a chair in front of my Bloods, I feel loved. I'm protected. Being here with them, my homees, I pour my problems out, getting strength in return. What we have is pure love and brotherhood. I trust these individuals with my life, for some have actually had a hand in saving it. I feel important in this circle. I am needed and understood. I have created what I have been searching for—a family.

Once the night filled with emotions, tears, and hugs is finally over, I spend my last precious moments with my baby girl. I know she wants to slap me because I can't stop kissing her. As she sleeps, I gaze at her. Such a pretty child, I think. There isn't a blemish on her honey-colored dimple face.

For the first time in my life, I pray for mercy.

On May 31, 2005, I go before Judge Vaughn for sentencing. As he prepares to render a decision that will determine my future, I can't fake, hide, or ignore my nervousness. Eleven months of stress and aggravation are at an end.

I fixate on Judge Vaughn's mouth as if I'm trying to pull the words directly out of him. I hate the fact that this White man who doesn't give a shit about me controls my future with the bang of his gavel. I think back on all the years my mom pleaded with me to stop gang banging.

"Straighten up, Dashaun, or you are going to end up dead or in jail." Damn, how often did I hear this at a time when I thought it wouldn't happen to me?

Sweat beads accumulate on my forehead with each excruciating tick of the clock. Seconds become hours. My heart begins to throb. Twenty minutes pass. Five minutes later, the judge instructs me to stand.

Judge Vaughn addresses me without looking at me. "Mr. Morris, you have been convicted of conspiracy and riot. Before I enter a sentence, is there anything that you would like to say?"

I stand up straight and look him directly in the eyes.

Honestly, I don't have shit to say. I want Joe to do the talking for me. I don't know how to come off remorseful because I'm not. Plus I won't beg for freedom, so instead I whisper to Joe.

"What should I say?" From here Joe takes the floor on my behalf and says things about me that make me think, *Who me?*

Judge Vaughn follows: "I can throw you in jail for a long time. But considering the agreement reached between your lawyer and the prosecutor, my decision will stay within the guidelines. However, I want you to understand something before I hand down this sentence. If I see you in my courtroom again you'll leave here a very old man." He points his index finger to add emphasis. "You are old enough to be responsible for your own actions." He stares at me waiting for a response. "Do we understand one another?" I nod. He moves some paperwork around as if he's looking for his answer to my sentence. I take another deep breath as he gives it to me.

"I hereby sentence you to three years level five suspended for six months, level five, suspended for two years, level three, suspended for six months, level two."

At first I don't know how much time this is so I whisper to my attorney, "How much time is that?"

"Six months."

*That's it! I can do this,* I reason. My stomach turns. I factor in my future for the next six months.

I feel anger and relief at the same time. I'm angry because I got bagged over a snitch. I'm relieved because six months is a small price not just here, but the whole life with the gang to pay for the charges I accumulated. I face Neina and my mother, who have tears in their eyes. Growing up banging and hustling, I always knew either death or jail was waiting its turn to embrace me.

As the bailiff escorts me out in handcuffs, my mom and Neina each give me a hug and kiss.

"We love you."

The hard part is finally over. I know how much time I have to do and I begin focusing on my bid.

My first day in the Delaware Correctional Center is one big mind game. I think to myself, *Who will I have to make an example of first?*

Stepping into DCC is like walking into a dark room with a spotlight on you. You are immediately escorted to the receiving room where you get your state whites.

Right away, I'm drilled by menacing-looking guards who make me strip ass naked. All of them are White. Once I'm completely naked they order me to stand in line for quite some time while they get up in my face and make all sorts of derogatory comments about me being a lowlife and how pitiful I am. They point out the fact that I'm not in Newark and that DCC is running things. They begin to body-search me, looking for weapons and contraband. They search up my rectum.

"Put your hands on top of your head. Show me under your arms. Open your mouth and move your tongue around. Turn around, bend over, spread your cheeks and cough. Let me see the bottom of your feet. Shake your hair around. Let me take a look at those nails."

I feel weak and trapped. My strength on the street is no match for the system. In the streets, a joker can't get in three words of disrespect, whereas in here, I'm constantly belittled and degraded. I have to take it. I hate it. I wanna show them who I am, how bad I can be, and that I ain't to be fucked with.

Following the search procedure, I'm transported to C Building. Walking down my wing feels eerie because I get crazy prison stares from every fool in each cell I pass along the way.

As I make my way down the tier, my street survival instincts kick in, and I find myself consciously looking for any known enemies I might have made in town. It's best if I spot them before they spot me. This way if I have to encounter a problem, I can be prepared to deal with it rather than allow myself to be caught slippin'. My experience with prison is limited but I have enough relatives who have been upstate to have heard the stories about the violence and how so many fools get rocked to sleep for not staying awake.

I'm relieved when I'm unable to recognize any potential threats, but I also know that I have to stay alert because DCC has two thousand prisoners.


My first night in DCC is long and lonely. I'm confined, forced to endure noise reaching riot level, lack of privacy, and strip searches. A feeling of anxiety, defeatism, aggravation, boredom, not to mention rodents and contagious diseases, is enough to drive anyone crazy. Panic. No light at the end of the tunnel. No way out of the bare, merciless walls. Inmates consumed by hatred and dread. I can hardly sleep at all the first night because the slab of metal I have to sleep on is so uncomfortable. Whichever side I lie on becomes numb. Getting used to this will eventually take its course but for now, it's nerve-racking. I toss and turn all night until I sit up in the bed resting against the back wall. This position too eventually becomes painful.

My mind races a hundred miles a minute, reflecting back on my life, the many things that I've done wrong, and how those behaviors ultimately led me to the predicament I'm in.

There are no amenities to speak of here. Not that I expect any privileges in the stark and desolate jail. I'm here to pay a debt to society; it's not supposed to be comfortable. But the average day in prison is painful. Endless torment by restriction and deprivation taunt us. Being told when to shower, eat, and sleep. Same faces, same smelly bodies packed together and treated like animals.

There's something about being locked down that can change a man and allow him to see the bigger picture. When one is confined in a six-by-nine cell for more than twenty hours a day, it affects your mental health. After a while, the cell walls start to close in on you and you start to experience a psychological perplexity.

When I recall my contributions to the gang, all I see is the Blood oozing from the bodies of my enemies. Suddenly guilt hits me and that sick feeling I had when I went on my first ride when I was eleven returns, spinning my stomach inside.

This is what separates me from many; inside my head is nothing but war. I hate to sleep. The darkness haunts me. I stay away from it. I joust between Dashaun and Machete; my mother's li'l boy and Machete the Blood, my brother's keeper. My opposing spirits fight each other in what feels like a never-ending battle for supremacy. I am Dr. Jekyll and Mr. Hyde.

I never understood why Mama made my younger brother and me go to church. I couldn't understand why she prayed to someone we could never see, hear, or touch, but yet had all the power in the world. Where I lived, all the power belonged to the guys with the guns and drugs. I couldn't trust in what I couldn't see, smell, taste, hear, or feel. My entire life I witnessed the power of life and death in the mercy or wrath of men and boys.

After being moved around through the Charlie, MHU, and Delta housing units, I end up in Victor. Living on the compound is a lot different than it was during Pre-Trial days. Pre-Trial inmates are rowdier and more aggressive, whereas compound has more of the prison-style code of living.

Out on the grounds, I immediately notice that all the prison guards and administrators are White, yet about 85 percent of the inmates are Black. I realize that the White prisoners stay to themselves and don't socialize with the Blacks.

Here in V Building, I meet Jersey. He's from Atlantic City. We eventually become tight and stick together during yard. I learn a lot from the brother in the short time we spend together. Jersey is Muslim and he's trying to get his life on track too. We discover that our moms have similar backgrounds and he introduces me to Islam.

Yard time is where I get to spread my wings and stay mobile. While working out, a Chicano stares at me. I'm aware of it when I finish up a set of dips and I hear a name called. When I turn to find the voice, I spot Lopez staring at me. He stands about five foot six, weighs maybe 170 pounds. He reminds me of the Mexicans I knew in Phoenix, with tattoos that cover most of his body and a bald head with a full beard that makes him look like a stone-cold killer. He poses a tough stance with his state pants pulled up high over his waist, damn near touching the top of his abs. I look past him and resume my workout. I can still feel him eyeing me. At my first opportunity I step to the Chicano, surprising him.

"Wass hannin' Blood, you know me?"

Considering my five or six inches in height hovering over the smaller Chicano, he's no match for me. Then reality flashes across my mind.

*I'm in prison, this is a fucking Mexican, and fighting is secondary to hawking people.* I store away the recognizable confidence and opt not to underestimate the smaller individual.

"You a Blood home bwoy?" he asks.

"Every day, why? Wass bangin'?" I respond with a slow lethargic pause after I slap on my gangsta mask. At this point we stare at each other for what seems forever.

"I'm Lopez from the 13s."

In the minds of the Sureno 13s, Bloods fall on the enemy side because we wear red and they wear blue. I remember Taz telling me Bloods got into beef with the 13s.

I suppose he learns of my affiliation by way of prison talk. You can't hide who you are in prison, and what you are classifies you as enemy or connected.

"What's ya angle like homez?"

He wants to know if I come in peace. I came to prison after this Blood and Mexican thing took off, so he has the jump on me and the ball is now in my court. Keeping in mind I don't know all the details of the beef, I'm reluctant to strike and instead issue a peace offering. While doing so, I make sure I maintain my aggressive posture so I don't convey weakness.

"I come in peace if you are?" At the same time I take one step back so as to position myself in a better defensive stance.

"It's peace homez; I ain't tryin' to be beefin' with no Bloods."

Naturally, I don't have any genuine hate for the homee so I agree to the treaty and, first chance I get, I break the news to the Bloods.

My sentence having kicked in, I know I won't be going home for a few months. I continue to think about all that I've done in my life and question my decisions.

Hearing the C/O call out names for mail, I hear my name. It's T. Rodgers writing me. I'm excited. T. Rodgers, a pivotal factor in uniting Bloods in the early seventies, challenges me to live for family and not die for homees. He writes: "You must gain peace, and by doing so, you first must forgive your enemies, and then forgive yourself. The greatest revenge is to live well." That day, he took me in as his son and changed my life. I confide in him. His letters to me in prison were the beginning of a relationship that I now hold sacred. T. Rodgers is a father figure in my life, a man that has done it all in the streets and now chooses to live better. He has taught me enormous lessons about life skills, as well as how to be a better father and man. I am forever grateful to him. And I know that, through our bond, he is blessed also. I am proud to be one that he trusts with his life, who he reaches out to when he is in need, and treats me with the love, respect, and honor of a son. Now and forever he is "my pops" T. Rodgers.

Living day in and day out, banging wears you down. I know going through this legal fight exposed me to the unpredictability of the streets and changed me tremendously. To see what it did to my family after all these years had a deep effect on me. All the hurt, pain, and sadness they feel every day make me feel I'm being selfish toward them. How can I truly say I love my daughter if my everyday actions put my freedom and life in jeopardy? Before my daughter, this didn't register, but after her birth, the lights turned on. I need to grow up. What point am I trying to prove by still bangin'?

In prison, time is all you have, a lot of idle time, and hardly anybody that you can trust. If you're not careful about whom you spend your time with and how you develop as a person, you can come out a worse individual than when you went in. I don't want that. I am ready to make the most of my time here; I'm open to changing, and challenging myself to become a better person.

One day at yard, I breathe the air, enjoying all the sun I can get. Birds fly overhead by the dozens. Strolling across the yard, I'm lost in thought. I see two men playing chess. I walk toward them, my eyes locked on the board. A man in his fifties, with jet-Black hair and a long beard, steals his opponent's queen. He speaks. "Give me that bitch! Moving too fast, you should have put your knight there, checked me, and stole my bitch." After a few more moves, he calls out checkmate. Game over.

Now waiting for his next vic, he motions for me to sit. He introduces himself. "I'm Muhammad." He has strong hands.

"Machete."

"That's what ya mama named you?"

"That's what I go by, Machete."

"You know how to push, Machete?" he asks.

I'm a beginner, but I can't tell him this.

"Fa' sho."

Playing chess with Muhammad, he drops jewels on me. He teaches me the power of chess, the game of life.

After a few moves, he can tell I bluffed my way into the game.

"You have to watch the entire board, young Blood. Not just your side, but mine too. You gotta be dynamic, good visualization and foresight."

Muhammad captures my rook.

"Identifying schemes will keep you ahead of your opponent and help you decipher his plans. Once you can pick your opponent apart, you can fashion tricks to counteract his offense. Chess is the game of life."

My queen captures his knight. Muhammad watches.

"See this is exactly what I'm trying to teach you, I baited you with that knight because you're thinking small.

"Check.

"In life you can't just jump at everything that looks good. I disguised a bad thing for you with a good-looking knight. There are consequences for every move you make in life. Just like chess." He looks me square in the eyes as he inches closer. I feel he knows my life story. "Never make a move before weighing the consequences. If you do, you can make a deadly mistake.

"Checkmate!"


Back in my cell, lying on my bed, I let Muhammad's words resonate. *In life you can't just jump at everything that looks good.* He's right. My whole life, that's exactly what I've done. I cliqued up with the set and vowed to be a rider without looking down the board. The consequences for that decision still haunt me to this day.

I sit night after night in my cell at midnight trying to lose myself in mindless television or sitting with the flickering light in my face thinking, *How did I make it all the way to college and end up in prison?* Inside, I wonder how different my experiences are from everyone around me. If I look at winning and losing, I don't see much difference at all. We're all here doing time and suffering the repercussions of our actions. I see some differences, and at times, I want to be better. I don't want to be recognized as an average man. I want to be more. Is that wrong? Is it wrong to want to be better than some of those around me? Sometimes, all I see is what can only be described as losers—those who refuse to win—those who let ambition slip away into the darkness, never to be found again. It's so frustrating when I think about it, I'm not frustrated about all the losers around me, I'm frustrated with all the loser that's in me. It's like my life story, I start out in the ghetto, go to college, and end up in prison. I repeat this process every day and with everything that I do. I start with little or nothing, work really hard at whatever it is that I set my mind to, diligently seeking out as many ways as I can to destroy it.

I am a fallen man, on my knees and deathly afraid. I am at the bottom, with nowhere to go except up. Some days I move forward a little and some days I take giant leaps. Other days aren't as good and I wake up in the morning near the bottom. Climbing out, up from the bottom, are the days I remember the most. Those are the most volatile days; the times that require I take the biggest leaps forward. I have to overcome so many fears, and the fear of being different is one of them. So many times in my life, that is what has held me back. And it's really weird. I know it's good for me to be myself and believe that I am doing what is right. But I also know myself and I am aware that if I am not grounded, if I am not rooted in the cement and secure in myself at any given time, I am susceptible to the many pressures around me, especially from my peers.

So really, I don't want to be better than anyone, I just want to feel a part of everyone. I just want to be accepted.

I'm learning so much about myself while locked up. Through regular meetings with my counselor, Ms. Gatlin, I am able to work on a lot of my personal issues and develop tools to help me manage my feelings. I am empowered and very lucky. I have access to a professional I can trust because I know she has faith in my ability to live a life destined for greatness. Now I believe it myself.

Near the end of my prison stay, I submit an editorial in the prison paper under a fictitious name. It's about the failure of the prison system to reform people and about my own plans to walk the straight and narrow. Part of it says:

The prison system, prior to my lockdown, is one of punish-ment and corruption, with public pronouncements of rehabil-itation. Now, after being in the belly of the beast, I do not alter my concept one iota. The system's full of moral impoverishment from the crooked C/O walking the tiers hassling inmates all the way up to the warden. There hasn't been any change in the system since I've been on the inside. I reveal this as a point of reference for the many that are misled about the truth and inadequacies of the system. I am intelligent and educated enough to realize the system lives by the "Do as I say, not as I do" theory. They bring in drugs, shanks, sell them, and then bust you. Since rehabilitation is the last thing the system offers, each individual must want to change. Considering most of the inmates in here, motivation is sought and lost to hopelessness.

My time at DCC gives me much to be grateful for. The bonds I built there and the good times I had considering my circumstances left me with a few happy memories.

As the day comes for my release, I know I'm ready to be a better man in society. My whole life has led me to this moment. I have been blessed to emerge with a testimony, the story of my journey that has the power to change lives and potentially save kids from suffering as I have. That's why during this time in prison, I've been writing my story down, laying the foundation for a memoir that might help people do the hardest thing there is to do: change.

Most important, I know I have to be there for my daughter.

Today I'm going home. As I pack my bags I am mindful that I have to apply everything I've learned inside as ammunition to fight the war outside. It's the only way I can win. I have a new mission and commitment to help as many kids as I can avoid falling into gang culture. This is my destiny because I now know that there is no such thing as a gang LIFESTYLE. The reality is that bangin' is SUICIDAL.

With every loss we give and take, ultimately, we all end up losing.

Today I am a blessed man, who dedicates his life to change. And so, as I pack up my pen and notebook, and walk through the opening gates that lead to the outside world, I take a deep breath as the sun hits my face, for I'm walking into my second chance. And with each step putting prison further behind me, I choose a better LIFE.

*Killers on the payroll*
*We thought of ourselves as to be men*
*Many waited until we could choose the right color*
*The rest got down or became one with the ground*
*When we wore the color we defined that color*
*Fist would fly with the might of hate as its force*
*Laugh at us, our elders did*
*I guess going from the shoulders wasn't man enough*
*Good food it was not*
*Rotten the fruit was indeed it was poison*
*Love your color by taking the life of the other color*
*No surprise they got high before they took lives*
*Smart men kill for business never for fun*
*We all got paid different wages*
*Some paid by a brother's gratitude*
*Others in a crime partner's love*
*Many in the satisfaction of the kill*
*All paid dues to our union*
*Always as a counter for my dead homee's mother's tears*
*Every tear that left her face may another foul color get*
    *buried in the ground*
*Besides the cars, money, and the girl they had*
*I wanted*
*More than just I, jumped at the payroll*
*Never would things be the same*
*Bullets push out just as easy as they went in*
*Many teardrops and open caskets*
*Damn, look what we have done now*
*How were we showing love for our dead brother?*
*When we had to have lost love to kill another brother*
*Payment for the first I shed blood*
*No more 40-oz of Olde E*

*Split between me, the driver, and this fool in the back*
*Eyes open wide shut for the first time*
*If thoughts would have entered years before its time*
*Less would be dead*
*Funny how we receive payment for killing*
*For our color had to prosper*
*Greater was the payment for allowing the next man to live*
*Helping us grow is what I do now*

JASON DAVIS

# Epilogue

For many, my story may seem extreme or at times hard to read, but I'm just one example of what many of our children are faced with on the road to manhood. Many of you will see parts of yourselves stuck, as I was, in a life plagued by trauma, violence, drugs, prison, and death. But my message to you is one of hope and encouragement. Once you decide that you want to make a change, you can begin the process of pulling yourself up out of life's gutter and creating a better life.

As you journey with me through the pages of my life, you will come to understand that my story is only unique in that I lived to tell it and that I have an outlet to voice my pain. I did not write this book to glorify violence. To be completely honest, I've gotten nothing from gang banging except dead homes that I miss, obituaries, tattoos that constantly remind me of all the friends I buried, felonies that prevent me from getting certain jobs, and nightmares that torture me. I simply wrote my story the way I experienced it. Ultimately, it is my hope that reading this book will motivate parents to see beyond the end results of gang violence by focusing on what creates a gang member in the first place.

As you read my story, I'm sure you will be able to pinpoint many areas that sent me down a path of gangs, violence, drugs, and death. I personally feel that each of us must bear responsibility and commit to changing the destructive behavior we are all dealing with. We are dying at record-breaking rates, even our babies. We must redirect our resources, use every skill we have as individuals and as a community to create solutions that provide real results. We've been suffering for far too long and it's crazy to think that change can't start today. We have no more time to wait; the time to act is now. I am committed to doing my part, and I hope that many of you that read along will feel my struggle and unite with me in taking our lives back.

# Afterword

I walked out of the Delaware Correctional Center on October 31, 2005. Six months later I was allowed to be a speaker at a high school in Newark, New Jersey. I accepted. From the front of the class I watch a bit hesitantly as gang members file into the classroom. Westside High is one of the most feared and dangerous high schools in Essex County and Newark.

Most of the youngsters slouch in their seats with the look of "What's this guy got to tell me that I don't know?"

As I scanned the class I spot at least three individuals from my neighborhood, and many of the youngsters sport colors, bandannas, and tats all over their bodies including teardrops along with their sets plastered on their faces for the world to see. They all were brought here by Coach Hoop, who teaches at Westside High, and they were there to hear my story. I guess they thought I'd just rant-'n'-rave about my glory days running with the gang, colors, turf wars, and drugs. Little did they know, that was the old me and I brought a different message.

I must admit I was a bit nervous at first. Thinking to myself, "What can I say that doesn't glorify gang life but penetrates their minds with a message of hope?" There wasn't much difference from my teenage years with the gang and theirs. Same angry and wicked stares, some of hopelessness and others of "ride and die" pride for their neighborhood. Many of them were at a disadvantage from birth, being crack babies, and being born into violent, unstable, and hopeless families. But like myself, they read deeper than the saggy pants, tats, mad dog stares, and colors. I read their pain; I saw what they couldn't articulate but displayed: despair.

I knew that whatever came out of my mouth, I had to identify with them to hold their attention: speak their language and empathize with what their reality was. So as the final few youngsters filled their seats, I closed my eyes, took a few deep breaths, and asked God to give me the words to hurt and heal. I say hurt and heal because I wanted to speak to their truth, speak to their pains and strains, provoke their hurt and misery, pull out their emotions, and to top it off, bring them back up. Lifting them, inspiring them to fight their circumstances and choose to live.

Through much growing up, maturing, and sacrificing I didn't think was possible, I survived a time of emotional, physical, and psychological difficulties. Now I want to help others.

I began by introducing myself as Dashaun "Jiwe" Morris. Many of them were already curious about me from reading my book or from word of mouth. Inside I immediately felt a tug of war because initially I was going to greet them with "Wassup lil homees," but I chose to say, "God bless all of you that showed up." After saying that—something I, for one, have never said in my life, let alone in a room full of bangers—an enormous amount of peace covered me. In my talk, I told them, "I was much of everything a YG wanted to be, and most likely wouldn't live long enough to become what I wanted to become. But as I stand before you all today, I come not as a gangster but as a man."

Now, having their attention, I saw a couple of faces with looks like "yeah right." That was cool, though. By the time I was done speaking, I knew I could win them over. I told them all that I had acquired in my years of active banging, such as street power and money. I also told them all the things I had lost, such as friends I had to bury, my NFL career, education, and ultimately *myself*. And third, I focused on how I was living my life today. I told them about things in life they hadn't experienced, trips I took, people I met, things they could become, and finally about the man I had become. I wanted them to feed off my perseverance and their reactions told me they were. This is the message I wanted them to hold on to and the life story I wanted to tell you.

# Acknowledgments

Acknowledgments are hard to write because I know I will leave out some important people. So before I begin, I humbly ask, that if I forget to mention you, charge it to my brain and not my heart.

First, I'd like to give thanks to God, who gave me strength in a time when I was drowning in an ocean of death. Thank you for allowing this to be possible.

## MY FAMILY

My #1 fan and eternal friend, my mother, **Andrea,** for giving me life, raising me as a single parent, and for always remaining in my corner, supporting me full throttle. When I look back at our history and how things transpired in my life, I can only say it was meant to happen that way. Without it, this book wouldn't exist, thank you. I love you and hope I've made you proud as a son.

My soul mate and backbone, **Neina,** for pushing me when I had nothing left in the tank. Never once have you faded away from my side, whenever I needed a shoulder to lean on, to get anger off my chest, or simply someone to talk to. You are a beautiful woman both inside as well as out. What you did for me many women wouldn't have had the patience to endure, and in return you have my heart and soul for life.

My pride and joy, **Da-Shana, Da-Sharie,** and **Da-Shani,** it is because of the three of you that Daddy is able to continue to fight every day. With the grace of God, you three give me my strength. Daddy loves you, and I hope that one day you can look back at my life and be proud of what your father did with it. *Nakupenda.*

To my godson **Dashaun Lofland.** One day when you're older you'll understand why things happened the way they did. But I've never forgotten you, and I think about you every day. I keep a picture of you in my wallet, and in my heart, you are my son. One day soon, you'll get to meet your two sisters. They'll be waiting. *Nakupenda.*

The entire **Morris and Bruce families,** too many to name, but I love y'all to death. To my older brother David, I'm glad we have reconnected. Big Daddy, who always has a spot at the crib for me whenever I'm in town. Aunt Claudette, for always supporting my family. My nieces and nephews, Aasha, Alana, Najee, Tykwan, Nasir, and Malachi. To the rest of the family, thanks for the encouragement and for accepting me the way I am.

The **Stewart family, Jeff, Grandma Gloria, Grandma Fegan, Carolyn, May-May, Lauren, Jay-Jay, Lisha, Devona, Shelly, Maliah, Laura,** and **Dano.**

**T. Rodgers.** I've learned so much about becoming a man from you that I wanna say thank you again. All the late-night conversations on the phone, I'll never forget them. The red-carpet treatment I get when I come to L.A. and the time we kick it and cook out in the Jungles are priceless. Like I always say, you represent to me what the absolute man is, and it's an honor and privilege to walk in your tracks.

**Coach Hoop,** thank you for stepping in, helping to mold me into a man. It's an honor to have someone as respected and real as you in my corner. You are definitely worthy of the father of the year award every day of your life. Thanks, Coach.

## MY DREAM TEAM

I'd like to give it up to a few people who made this book physically possible.

**Terrie M. Williams,** my agent, for your vision of what this book would do from the very beginning. You had it all mapped out. Thanks for leading and guiding me. I've learned so much from you on a business tip and personal level. You symbolize what a nurturer should be, taking someone from little next to nothing and making it shine. Thank you, Terrie, I'm rollin' wit'cha till da wheels fall off.

**Elizabeth Wareham,** my editor at Scribner. I want to thank you for giving me the opportunity for my story to be heard. Thank you for the many hours we spent on the phone getting it together. I remember you pushing me to write the best book I could. Despite your terrible taste in football teams (Cowboys), you are a special person to me, and I'm glad our paths crossed. Thank you for taking a chance on me and believing in my words.

I want to also thank Simon & Schuster CEO **Carolyn Reidy,** Scribner publisher **Susan Moldow, Kate Bittman, John Fulbrook, Whitney Frick, Brian Belfiglio, Tyler Lebleu,** and **Kathleen Rizzo** for the remarkable job done on producing this book. This was truly a team effort. Thank you all.

**Madeline McCray,** where do I begin? Many thanks for the love and support you constantly throw my way. You are an amazing woman and I am grateful to have you in my life.

**David Grand,** my psychotherapist. Our discussions as well as your continued support have been priceless to me. Thank you.

## My Support Group

You have been there for me to turn to, offering me your time, resources, and trust.

**Ms. Edna Piper** and **Connie Hall,** throughout all my legal troubles in Delaware, you two were the only ones that continued to believe in me. You didn't turn your backs on me like many others did. I'll never forget it and I hope to have made you two beautiful women proud. Thank you.

**Dr. Wendal Gorum,** you provided me with guidance and your finances. You were right there beside me throughout the whole ordeal. I genuinely respect you.

**Nicole Gould,** these words are meant to express my gratitude for you. To me, you symbolize the true meaning of a friend. Through some of my roughest times, you were there, giving me comfort and your support. Thank you.

My legal eagles who have helped me remain a free man: **Brook Barnett, Gerald Saluti** (NJ), you've been phenomenal in all that you've done for me; I truly appreciate it and you; **Stan Mitchell** (PA), **Joseph Hurley** (DE), and **Glenn** from Right Away bonds. I appreciate all of you.

To my good friend **Ilyasah Shabazz,** it has been an honor to work with you on a business level, and even more to have become friends with you on a personal level. You have been extremely helpful to me and I thank you. *Salaam!*

**Angie Daniels,** who before I even signed a deal, before even meeting me, began editing my book. I will always hold that in the highest and will always respect you full throttle.

Collectively, I wanna thank all of you from the circle of support brought to me by **Terrie M. Williams: Susan Taylor, Terry McMillan, Ed Dowdy, Loreen Arbus, Maggie Craddock, Alan Gansberg, Natatia Griffith, Shawn Dove, Curtis Bunn, Steve Perry, Dana Roc, Cheryl Duncan,** and **Carol Jones.** Thank you all.

## MY HOMEES

Infinite love goes out to all the street tribes who've lost soldiers. Think not that all the deaths we've suffered over the years have been in vain; let's use them as a stepping stone to ensure longevity in the future for our li'l ones. With this book, we now have a voice that must be heard. So much pain and torment we go through. We need in on a better life for ourselves and those that depend on us. I believe in you all. I salute all of you. Peace followed by a clenched fist from your brother Jiwe.

To the brothers still locked down behind the G-wall, my highest salutes and prayers are with you every night before my eyes get heavy. Keep fighting for ya freedom.

## MY READERS

I cannot end this without giving special thanks to my readers. Spreading this story, my message, would not be possible if you did not read it. May my words in this book help motivate you to make a positive change. I personally thank each and every one of you for buying into a piece of my life. I appreciate all the calls, e-mails, and constant support I've received since the release of my memoir.

For those that wanna holla at me, or tell me what you think and feel after reading the book, I am reachable.

(609) 503-3056

il: warofthebloods@jiweera.com

bsite: www.jiweera.com

Pain is profit!
Jiwe Era!

To book me for speaking engagements, contact me via the information above.

*War of the Bloods in My Veins* has been optioned by a production company and is being developed as a major motion picture.